MAP OF PHILIPPINES

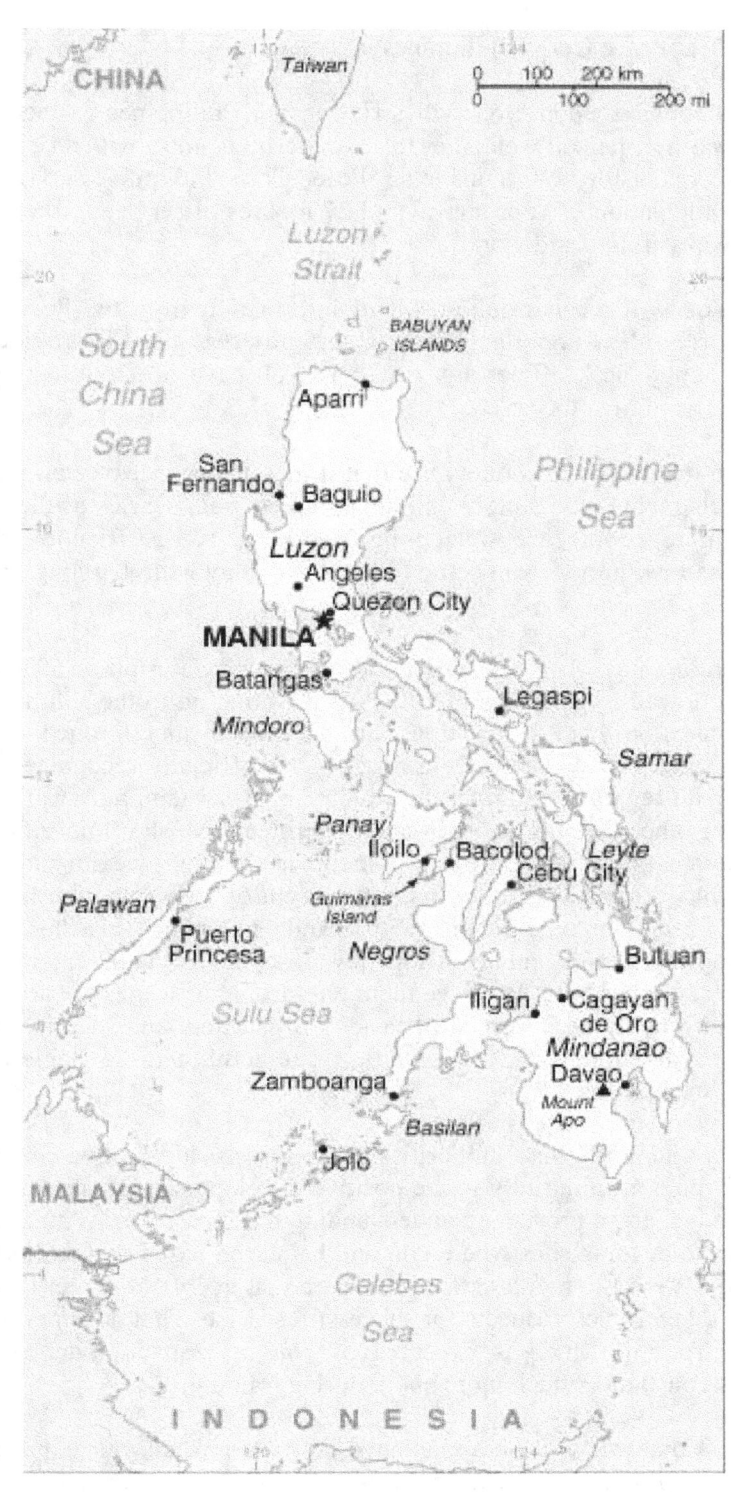

A WELCOME LETTER

Dear Peace Corps/Philippines invitee,

Mabuhay! Soon, you will arrive in the Philippines to receive the first of many warm in-person welcomes to a wonderful country with a rich and productive Peace Corps history. With this letter, Peace Corps/Philippines invites you to join us in our anticipation of your arrival and 27 months of service to the communities in which you will live and work.

You will receive quite a bit of information from the Peace Corps prior to your arrival. It is important that you carefully read what is provided to you and ask the country desk officer any questions you have prior to making the very important commitment to serve.

Peace Corps service, no matter when in one's life that it may happen, leaves an indelible and cherished impression upon one's character. You simply will not complete your service as the same person who will start training. The Filipino people are welcoming, generous, warm, friendly, and resourceful. The relationships you will share with those you come to know will stay with you long, long after your service is completed.

How to describe the Philippines? The colloquial and oft-quoted description of the Philippines is "350 years of Spanish rule followed by 50 years of Hollywood," alluding to the significant influence of both Spain and the United States on this Asian nation. But that only begins to touch on the many social and cultural layers you'll discover here. There are a dizzying 87 officially recognized languages and many more dialects spoken. With regard to religion, the country is overwhelmingly Catholic with a significant and growing presence of other denominations—and a significant Muslim minority, largely in the south. The economy is a study in contrasts: extreme (and sometimes alarming) wealth and poverty with a serious income-distribution problem that leaves more than 50 percent of the population living (or *trying* to live) on less than $2 a day. The geography is diverse, with islands, mountains, beaches, and vast plains of rice fields. The climate is tropical, humid, and hot, with a few oases of cool in the mountains up north. Natural disasters are frequent occurrences here: We have them all—from hurricanes to earthquakes to tsunamis to volcanoes—and you will quickly be informed of Peace Corps safety and security measures to stay safe. The people are the best—welcoming, friendly, warm, resourceful, and the single most valuable part of virtually all Volunteers' experience.

Peace Corps/Philippines and Philippine authorities place a very high value on the potential of each Volunteer, both to contribute meaningfully to the positive development of people in a community and to gain experience, knowledge, and a broadened understanding during service. With these goals in mind, our staff team work together to develop sites where you will be placed based on your individual skills and the needs of the community. We make a great effort to ensure that every Volunteer has a well-defined, full-time job where you have favorable prospects for successful service. That does not mean we have cleared the path entirely—far from it! Much is expected of you in terms of adaptability, flexibility, and resiliency—three words you'll hear much more about during training.

Becoming a productive Volunteer will be a challenge no matter what your experience, background, or age. Pre-service training will equip you with an array of skills and integration strategies, but how you apply those at site will be up to you. The efforts you put into practicing the local language and the time you spend building relationships at the beginning of your service will reap great benefits as you continue.

One of the most enduring and stunning characteristics of Peace Corps service is how it is both a communal and deeply individual experience. The diversity of Americans serving with the Peace Corps around the globe strengthens us. Each of you will contribute to the diversity of your group, and you will demonstrate both to each other and your host country partners how our nation's diversity creates our ever evolving culture. Your journey will be as individual as you are. Our staff of Americans and Filipinos is dedicated to supporting you on the journey.

Your first three months in-country will be filled with new experiences including structured language, technical, safety and security, and intercultural instruction as well as hands-on experience. You will need to demonstrate your readiness to adhere to the Core Expectations of Peace Corps Volunteers (listed after the Table of Contents). As fair warning, the Peace Corps has lots of rules. All are intended to ensure you and your peers' successful and safe service.

Your training will include living with a Filipino family. You will be expected to participate in normal daily activities as well as family and community events. Do not be surprised to find yourself the center of unusual interest. For those of you who may have lived independently for a while, family life may be quite an adjustment. It is, however, the very best way to integrate into your community. We replicate the host family living experience when you begin your service as a PCV at your permanent site. For the first three months you will be hosted by a family who will introduce you to your new community and help build your language and cultural awareness skills. Many PCVs choose to continue to live with host families throughout their service.

On behalf of the entire Peace Corps/Philippines staff, all of whom are excited to meet you and busy preparing for your arrival, congratulations on your invitation. Thank you in advance for your desire and commitment to serve and to begin this life-changing journey with us.

Sincerely,

Jean E. Seigle
Country Director

TABLE OF CONTENTS

CORE EXPECTATIONS FOR PEACE CORPS VOLUNTEERS

In working toward fulfilling the Peace Corps mission of promoting world peace and friendship, as a trainee and Volunteer, you are expected to do the following:

1. Prepare your personal and professional life to make a commitment to serve abroad for a full term of 27 months
2. Commit to improving the quality of life of the people with whom you live and work and, in doing so, share your skills, adapt them, and learn new skills as needed
3. Serve where the Peace Corps asks you to go, under conditions of hardship if necessary, and with the flexibility needed for effective service
4. Recognize that your successful and sustainable development work is based on the local trust and confidence you build by living in, and respectfully integrating yourself into, your host community and culture
5. Recognize that you are responsible 24 hours a day, 7 days a week for your personal conduct and professional performance
6. Engage with host country partners in a spirit of cooperation, mutual learning, and respect
7. Work within the rules and regulations of the Peace Corps and the local and national laws of the country where you serve
8. Exercise judgment and personal responsibility to protect your health, safety, and well-being and that of others
9. Recognize that you will be perceived in your host country and community as a representative of the people, cultures, values, and traditions of the United States of America
10. Represent responsibly the people, cultures, values, and traditions of your host country and community to people in the United States both during and following your service

PEACE CORPS/PHILIPPINES HISTORY AND PROGRAMS

History of the Peace Corps in Philippines

Peace Corps/Philippines is the agency's second-oldest country program. In October 1961, the first group of Peace Corps Volunteers arrived in Manila to work throughout the country as English language, mathematics, and science teachers. Since then, more than 8,800 Peace Corps Volunteers have served in the Philippines.

Beginning in the 1970s, Peace Corps/Philippines decreased the education component of its program and focused on social and economic development in rural areas. Volunteers worked on projects in health and nutrition, appropriate technology, water sanitation, agricultural extension, marketing cooperatives, fisheries, income generation, agroforestry, upland community development, vocational education, deaf education, local development planning, and small business development.

From the mid-1980s through the '90s, Volunteers once again worked in schools, this time as teacher trainers at the high-school level, while others were assigned to projects in health, agriculture, fisheries, agroforestry, income generation, and local development planning.

In June 1990, the Peace Corps suspended the Philippines program due to security concerns. The program resumed in 1992 with Volunteers working in coastal resources management, health and nutrition, water sanitation, and local development planning. In the past decade, the Peace Corps has sustained a strong programmatic commitment to environmental protection while also focusing on academic education and assistance to particularly vulnerable Filipinos.

At present, 180 Volunteers work alongside Filipino counterparts to teach students and train teachers; strengthen organizations working with children, youth, and families at risk; and assist communities in the management and conservation of coastal resources.

Peace Corps Programming in the Philippines

Peace Corps/Philippines has sustained a strong programmatic commitment to three areas: environmental protection, education and literacy, and youth development with an emphasis on particularly vulnerable Filipinos.

English Education Volunteers co-teach with Filipino teachers in elementary schools, high schools, colleges, and universities. The education sector aims to improve English language proficiency and teaching, raise academic performance of students, and increase school community participation. A number of Volunteers also co-teach at the tertiary level. Volunteers serve in community learning centers through the Alternative Learning Center.

Children, Youth, and Family Services (CYF) Volunteers work in government social welfare centers and faith-based and nongovernmental organizations that develop and educate at-risk children, youth, and families. Volunteers in this project work with children in conflict with the law; abandoned, neglected, and abused children and youth; and children and adults with physical and mental disabilities. CYF Volunteers also participate in the 4Ps Program (Pantawid Pamilyang Pilipino Program or Conditional Cash Transfer Program), a national anti-poverty program where the poorest families may be eligible for monthly stipends.

Coastal Resource Management (CRM) Volunteers assist coastal communities' efforts to implement restoration and protection of marine habitats and to enhance food security through participative community action and environmental education. They work with local government units to implement integrated CRM plans, assist communities with environmental education and training, and establish the bases for legal protection of fish stocks and marine habitats. Although environmental education is a core function of the CRM sector, it is very much people-centered and participatory in its approach to conservation and sustainable use of coastal and marine resources.

Peace Corps/Philippines also hosts one of the largest Peace Corps Response programs worldwide, utilizing short-term, high-impact Volunteers to deepen technical expertise with consideration to host country needs. Response Volunteers compliment the three sectors where two-year Volunteers are serving. The program in the Philippines has had ranged from 15 to 37 Response Volunteers in any given year, and continues to grow.

COUNTRY OVERVIEW: PHILIPPINES AT A GLANCE

History

The first people known to inhabit the Philippines are believed to have crossed over land bridges from Asia between 30,000–60,000 years ago, bringing with them knowledge of rice cultivation techniques that are still in practice. Later, they were joined in the Philippine archipelago by successive waves of Malay and Polynesian settlers who arrived in boats and formed small communities throughout the islands.

By the time the Spanish invasions began in the early 16th century, Chinese, Arab, and other immigrants had also arrived in the Philippines and contributed their bloodlines and cultures to the Asian-Pacific mosaic that characterizes Philippine society today. Immigration from other Asian countries continued during the 19th and 20th centuries, and the Philippines is currently experiencing notable influxes of Korean and Japanese people seeking sunny weather and business opportunities.

Ferdinand Magellan's attempt to circumnavigate the world ended in April 1521 in a battle near a small island off Cebu. Through this first European incursion into the Philippines, Spain claimed the archipelago, which eventually led to more than three centuries of Spanish rule.

Most Filipinos converted to Roman Catholicism and other Christian denominations during Spanish and American rule. Ardent Christianity is a principal and pervasive feature of Philippine national life, and even members of the Muslim minority often are educated in Christian schools and colleges.

Independence from Spain was declared by Filipino nationalists on June 12, 1898. However, the United States simultaneously occupied Manila during the Spanish-American War, and almost a half century of American colonial administration began. Japan conquered the islands during World War II and then lost them to a joint American and Filipino invasion force that re-established American rule. The period after World War II saw U.S.-assisted reconstruction and independence on July 4, 1946.

From the mid-1960s to the mid-'80s, President Ferdinand Marcos dominated Philippine politics. This period included martial law and suspension of democratic institutions. The first "People Power" revolt toppled Marcos' regime in 1986. Corazon Aquino, the widow of Marcos' principal opponent, became president, and democratic institutions began functioning again. Fast forward to 2010: Following several administrations reflecting the political dynasties of the Philippines, the current president is Benigno "Noynoy" Aquino III, son of former President Aquino and assassinated political dissident, Benigno Aquino Jr. During his six-year term (which ends in 2016), many expect great improvement in governance.

Government

The Philippines has a constitutional government with a bicameral Congress. The president is elected directly by the voters. Administratively, the country is divided into 16 regions with 73 provinces, each with an elected governor. Municipalities, which are administered by elected mayors, consist of varying numbers "neighborhoods," called *barangays*.

At the local and national level, Philippine political power traditionally has been exercised by networks of leading families that often have difficulty differentiating between their personal interests and their responsibilities under the Philippine Constitution to conduct the public's business accountably. An ordinary Filipino who lacks the backing of a powerful patron can experience hardships in gaining access to educational, employment, or business opportunities.

Economy

The Philippine economy grew rapidly after World War II but slowed in the 1950s and was hit with a severe economic recession from 1984–85. Despite this setback, infrastructure improvements, including paved roads, electrification, water supply, and other public facilities, were completed throughout most of the Philippines and in the 1990s, economic growth accelerated somewhat.

In recent years, the economy of the Philippines has picked up considerably, and primary exports include semiconductors and electronic products, transport equipment, garments, copper products, petroleum products, coconut oil, and fruits. The GDP annual growth rate for 2013 is estimated at almost 7 percent and currently ranks as one of the fastest growing economies in Southeast Asia.

Even with this promising outlook, the performance of the Philippine economy continues to favor those who are educated, well connected, and live in urban areas. The urban poor and the majority of people in rural areas struggle against formidable odds to gain a living. This, combined with rapid population growth, has produced widespread joblessness and historically high levels of labor migration out of the country.

People and Culture

The Philippines is a nation of approximately 100 million people living on an archipelago made up of 107 islands, or roughly the size of Arizona. Around 80 percent of the Philippine population identifies as Christian. Ten percent are Muslims, and the rest practice other religions or none at all.

In comparison to its Southeast Asian neighbors, Filipino food is not particularly spicy, but it does share rice as a common staple. Popular dishes include adobo, which is a meat stew made from either pork or chicken, vinegar, soy sauce, black peppercorns, and garlic. Other dishes include *lumpia*, a meat or vegetable roll; *pancit* (noodle); and *lechon* (roasted pig). Filipinos typically eat with a fork and a spoon, and sometimes with their hands.

The national sport is *arnis*, a form of martial arts. As a result of the American-Filipino connection, basketball has become one of the most popular sports to watch and play. Video-ke is also a common pastime and popular at parties.

The Philippines is a veritable melting pot of cultures: Asian, Spanish, and American influences have pervaded everyday life. These influences are seen throughout the people and culture of the country and contribute to the uniqueness of this island nation.

RESOURCES FOR FURTHER INFORMATION

Following is a list of websites for additional information about the Peace Corps and Philippines and to connect you to returned Volunteers and other invitees. Please keep in mind that although the Peace Corps tries to make sure all these links are active and current, the Peace Corps cannot guarantee it. If you do not have access to the Internet, visit your local library. Libraries offer free Internet usage and often let you print information to take home.

A note of caution: As you surf the Internet, be aware that you may find bulletin boards and chat rooms in which people are free to express opinions about the Peace Corps based on their own experiences, including comments by those who were unhappy with their choice to serve in the Peace Corps. These opinions are not those of the Peace Corps or the U.S. government, and please keep in mind that no two people experience their service in the same way.

General Information About the Philippines

State.gov
The Department of State's website issues background notes periodically about countries around the world. Find Philippines and learn more about its social and political history. You can also go to the site's international travel section to check on conditions that may affect your safety.

Gpo.gov/libraries/public/
The U.S. Government Printing Office publishes country studies intermittently.

lcweb2.loc.gov/frd/cs/cshome.html
The Library of Congress provides historical and sociological data on numerous countries.

http://unstats.un.org/unsd/pocketbook/World_Statistics_Pocketbook_2013_edition.pdf
United Nations resource book with 2013 statistical country data

Data.un.org
United Nations site with links to data from U.N. member countries

Wikipedia.org
Search for Philippines to find encyclopedia-type information. Note: As Wikipedia content is user-generated, information may be biased and/or not verified.

Worldbank.org
The World Bank Group's mission is to fight poverty and improve the living standards of people in the developing world. It is a development bank that provides loans, policy advice, technical assistance, and knowledge-sharing services to developing countries to reduce poverty. This site contains a lot of information and resources regarding development.

Data.worldbank.org/country
Provides information on development indicators on countries, including population, gender, financial, education, and climate change statistics.

Connect With Returned Volunteers and Other Invitees

RPCV.org
This is the site of the National Peace Corps Association, made up of returned Volunteers. On this site you can find links to all the Web pages of the "Friends of" groups for most countries of service, comprised of former Volunteers who served in those countries. There are also regional groups that frequently get together for social events and local volunteer activities.

PeaceCorpsWorldwide.org
This site, hosted by a group of returned Volunteer writers, is a monthly online publication of essays and Volunteer accounts of their Peace Corps service.

http://www.rpcvphilippines.org/
Peace Corps Philippines Alumni Foundation for Philippine Development is run by RPCVs who served in the Philippines over the past 40 years. The foundation provides scholarships for promising Filipinos in financial need.

Online Articles/Current News Sites About Philippines

UN.org/News/
The United Nations news service provides coverage of its member states and information about the international peacekeeping organization's actions and positions.

VOAnews.com
Voice of America, the U.S. government's multimedia broadcaster, features coverage of news around the world.

www.inquirer.net
The site of the Philippine Daily Inquirer

www.mb.com.ph
Manila Bulletin website

www.philstar.com
Philippine Star website

http://manila.usembassy.gov/
U.S. Embassy in the Philippines

Philippine Government Agencies

www.dti.gov.ph
Philippines Department of Trade and Industry

www.pia.gov.ph
Philippines Information Agency

www.deped.gov.ph
Department of Education

www.neda.gov.ph
National Economic and Development Authority

www.denr.gov.ph
Department of Environment and Natural Resources

www.doh.gov.ph
Department of Health

www.dswd.gov.ph
Department of Social Welfare and Development

International Development Sites About the Philippines
www.who.int
World Health Organization

www.imf.org/external/country/phl/index.htm
International Monetary Fund

http://www.usaid.gov/philippines
U.S. Agency for International Development

www.mcc.gov
Millennium Challenge Corporation

http://www.adb.org/countries/philippines/main
Asian Development Bank

www.haribon.org.ph
Haribon Foundation for the Conservation of Natural Resources, a Philippine nonprofit that promotes environmental protection and sustainable resource management

Recommended Books

Books About the History of the Peace Corps
1. Hoffman, Elizabeth Cobbs. "All You Need is Love: The Peace Corps and the Spirit of the 1960s." Cambridge, MA: Harvard University Press, 2000.
2. Rice, Gerald T. "The Bold Experiment: JFK's Peace Corps." Notre Dame, IN: University of Notre Dame Press, 1985.
3. Stossel, Scott. "Sarge: The Life and Times of Sargent Shriver." Washington, DC: Smithsonian Institution Press, 2004.
4. Meisler, Stanley. "When the World Calls: The Inside Story of the Peace Corps and its First 50 Years." Boston: Beacon Press, 2011.

Books on the Volunteer Experience
1. Dirlam, Sharon. "Beyond Siberia: Two Years in a Forgotten Place." Santa Barbara, CA: McSeas Books, 2004.
2. Casebolt, Marjorie DeMoss. "Margarita: A Guatemalan Peace Corps Experience." Gig Harbor, WA: Red Apple Publishing, 2000.
3. Erdman, Sarah. "Nine Hills to Nambonkaha: Two Years in the Heart of an African Village." New York City: Picador, 2003.
4. Hessler, Peter. "River Town: Two Years on the Yangtze." New York City: Perennial, 2001.
5. Kennedy, Geraldine ed. "From the Center of the Earth: Stories out of the Peace Corps." Santa Monica, CA: Clover Park Press, 1991.
6. Thomsen, Moritz. "Living Poor: A Peace Corps Chronicle." Seattle: University of Washington Press, 1997 (reprint).

Books About the Philippines

1. Guerrero, Amadis. "The Philippines: A Journey Through the Enchanted Isles." Manila, Philippines: Anvil Publishing, 1995.
2. Hagedorn, Jessica. "Burning Heart: A Portrait of the Philippines." Rizzoli, 1999.
3. Joaquin, Nick. "Manila, My Manila." Makati City, Philippines: Bookmark, 1999.
4. Karnow, Stanley. "In Our Image: America's Empire in the Philippines." New York: Ballantine Books, 1990 (reissue edition).
5. Peters, Jens. "Philippines Travel Guide." Jens Peters Publications, 2005.
6. Rowthorn, Chris. "Philippines." Lonely Planet Publications, 2003.
7. Whitehead, Kendal. "Odyssey of a Philippine Scout: Fighting, Escaping and Evading the Japanese, 1941–1944." The Aberjona Press, 2006.

LIVING CONDITIONS AND VOLUNTEER LIFESTYLE

Communications
Mail
Letters sent by post usually take one to two weeks to arrive. They should be sent to the following:

"Your Name," PCT	**OR**	"Your Name," PCT
U.S. Peace Corps		c/o U.S. Peace Corps
P.O. Box 7013		6th Floor, PNB Financial Center
N.A.I.A.		Diosdado
Pasay City, Philippines		Macapagal Ave.
1301		Pasay City, Philippines
		1308

A Peace Corps staff member picks up the mail from the airport post office box regularly and sends it to Volunteer sites by special delivery through a courier service or through the Philippine mail system.
When the Peace Corps receives a package addressed to a Volunteer, the Volunteer is notified and asked for forwarding instructions. If a package is forwarded, the Volunteer is responsible for the cost.
After training, many Volunteers choose to have packages and letters mailed directly to their sites.
Please note that all mail sent through the above Peace Corps addresses is opened and checked according to standard U.S. government policy.

Peace Corps Volunteers regularly use the Philippine postal system without problems to send mail inexpensively to friends and family.

Peace Corps/Philippines advises you not to have packages sent through any airline. Even if the freight charges are prepaid in the United States, there will be numerous charges in the Philippines for customs, brokerage, storage, and clearing.

Telephones
Cellphone use is ubiquitous in the Philippines and is the standard form of communication between staff and Volunteers (texting is the preferred mode). Many Volunteers use cellphones for calls to and from the United States. The Peace Corps will issue every Volunteer a cellphone upon arrival in-country. If lost, the Volunteer is responsible for replacing it. The Peace Corps does not recommend that Volunteers bring their U.S. cellphones both due to the difficulty in operating as well as the appearance of wealth it conveys. Most Volunteers communicate with friends and family in the U.S. through Skype or other social networking media in addition to cellphones. In emergencies, it is best for families to call Peace Corps Counseling and Outreach Unit in Washington, D.C., at 855.855.1961 ext. 1470. They will immediately contact Peace Corps/Philippines staff, who will ensure that word gets to the Volunteer as soon as practicably possible.

Computer, Internet, and Email Access
Most Philippine cities and towns have Internet cafes and you will have access to some type of email, if not at your site, at least in a neighboring city. Connections can be slow, and Volunteers typically will usually only be able to conduct the most rudimentary of online business, e.g., email. Almost all Volunteers bring laptops or tablets and find them essential. Increasingly, there are hotspots for wireless (Wi-Fi) access in Manila and other major cities in the country. There are also mobile telephone options available to obtain Internet anywhere there is a signal. Having a laptop or tablet in the Philippines involves worries about humidity, fluctuating current, and the risk of theft. Any expensive electronic equipment should be insured for loss before arrival in the Philippines.

Housing and Site Location

Housing conditions for Volunteers vary widely depending upon their sites and can range from heavily urban to very rural. For Volunteers assigned to underdeveloped areas, housing typically is a hollow concrete block, wood, or bamboo structure. In more developed areas, housing can be either the same or more substantial. Most houses have running water and electricity.

Trainees live with host families during pre-service training and during the first three months at their assigned sites. Married Volunteers stay with separate host families during pre-service training. After this period, Volunteers may choose to continue living with a host family or to move into their own rented accommodations. Volunteers are strongly encouraged to continue living with host families. Usually the Volunteers who continue living with host families develop the best Philippine language fluency and the deepest understanding of Filipino culture.

Living Allowance and Money Management

Volunteers receive a monthly allowance in Philippine pesos that is sufficient to live at the level of the local people. The allowance covers food, housing, household supplies, clothing, transportation to and from work, utilities, recreation and entertainment, and incidental expenses. Peace Corps Volunteers are expected to live at a level that is comparable with that of their host country counterparts. The Peace Corps discourages Volunteers from supplementing their living allowance with funds from home.

ATM savings accounts are opened for all Volunteers immediately upon their arrival in the Philippines. These accounts are used for all deposits that Peace Corps/Philippines makes for Volunteers. ATMs are available in most major cities. Credit and debit cards should be carefully guarded against theft and scams.

Food and Diet

Rice is the staple food for most Filipinos who live in the lowlands, while corn, potatoes, and tubers are the staple foods of people who live at higher altitudes. Fish, pork, chicken, bread, noodles, various vegetables, bananas, and some other fruits are widely available. Food is often cooked in lard or coconut oil. Many Filipinos prefer rice, fish, meat, and sweets over vegetables and fruits. Maintaining a strict vegetarian diet can be difficult, and vegetarians need to expend considerable time and energy to maintain a healthy diet. Every region of the Philippines has its own specialty dishes and staple foods depending on the availability of local fruits and vegetables.

Transportation

In cities or municipalities, the most common means of transportation are buses and minibuses, including small trucks called "jeepneys" that usually are decorated in bright colors. Other transportation includes motorized tricycles and bicycle-powered carts called pedicabs. Travel among islands is via airplane, ship, or small motorboat. Peace Corps Volunteers are not allowed to own or operate any vehicle, and driving or riding on a motorcycle is strictly prohibited.

Geography and Climate

Weather in almost all parts of the Philippines is hot and humid year-round. The weather pattern is changeable, but it usually consists of a dry season from approximately January to June and a wet season for the remainder of the year. January is usually the coolest month, and May is the hottest. Higher elevations in some places are cooler year-round. Heavy rainfall occurs in all parts of the Philippines, and strong storms are frequent.

Social Activities

Many Filipinos are wonderfully gregarious and very adept at pleasant chats. Volunteers should be prepared for frequent and fascinating impromptu conversations in all manner of places. Quite personal questions from Filipinos can at times startle and amuse Americans who typically are more reserved.

Social events are an important part of Philippine life, and get-togethers of work colleagues and friends can start at a moment's notice. Typical occasions are mid-morning and mid-afternoon snacks called *merienda,* which may include pastries, rice dishes, noodles, spaghetti, and a lot more.

Volunteers often are invited to birthday parties, baptisms, weddings, blessings of new buildings, and programs to celebrate holidays and important school or local events. Each community holds an annual *fiesta* and residents take great pride in the elaborate preparations.

Volunteers are encouraged to be open to social contacts and to participate in social events whenever possible. Filipino colleagues, friends, and neighbors welcome Volunteers' participation in social events, and social occasions offer Volunteers both pleasant ways to relax and valuable opportunities to learn about Filipino customs and traditions.

Professionalism, Dress, and Behavior

Despite the considerable level of Western influence that Volunteers experience throughout the Philippines, Philippine culture generally is quite conservative. This is especially the case outside large cities. One aspect of this conservatism is the high priority that Filipinos place on a neat personal appearance. Volunteers, whether urban or rural-based, should wear neat and clean clothing at all times when they are in public and especially when they are at their worksites. Sloppiness, poor hygiene, and bad grooming can cause Filipinos to avoid a person. Such avoidance can effectively negate a Volunteer's chances of cooperating successfully at the workplace and interacting effectively with the people in the community.

Volunteers should always bear in mind that they are in the Philippines as professional development workers and not as backpacking world travelers. Appropriate dress will be discussed regularly during pre-service training and often includes feedback to Volunteers who may be accustomed to expressions of independence through wardrobe.

Personal Safety

More detailed information about the Peace Corps' approach to safety is contained in the Safety and Security section, but it is an important issue and cannot be overemphasized. As stated in the Volunteer Handbook, becoming a Peace Corps Volunteer entails certain safety risks. Living and traveling in an unfamiliar environment (oftentimes alone), having a limited understanding of local language and culture, and being perceived as well-off are some of the factors that can put a Volunteer at risk. Many Volunteers experience varying degrees of unwanted attention and harassment. Petty thefts and burglaries are not uncommon, and incidents of physical and sexual assault do occur, although most Philippines Volunteers complete their two years of service without incident. The Peace Corps has established procedures and policies designed to help reduce the risks and enhance your safety and security. These procedures and policies, in addition to safety training, will be provided once you arrive in the Philippines. Using these tools, one can be empowered to take responsibility for his or her safety and well-being.

Each staff member at the Peace Corps is committed to providing Volunteers with the support they need to successfully meet the challenges they will face to have a safe, healthy, and productive service. Volunteers and families are encouraged to look at safety and security information on the Peace Corps website at peacecorps.gov/safety.

Information on these pages gives messages on Volunteer health and safety. There is a section titled Safety and Security in Depth. Among topics addressed are the risks of serving as a Volunteer, posts' safety support systems, and emergency planning and communications.

Rewards and Frustrations

Daily life for vast numbers of Filipinos has long revolved around the occupations that occur in various seasons. One aspect of the strong rural cultural influence can be a lack of concern for punctuality and prompt follow through. For Filipinos, it seems there is always time, while for Westerners it may seem there is never enough time. Things do not necessarily happen as scheduled. Volunteers who are bothered by other people's tardiness or their failure to show up somewhere or produce something will need to develop patience in order to accept disappointment without anger.

Traditional Philippine kinship customs contribute to an easy attitude toward helping oneself to other people's personal possessions. This is especially true among family members. Sharing is common and not doing so is considered anti-social. If a Volunteer wishes to keep any item entirely to him- or herself, lock it away out of sight.

Previously, issues relating to American military bases in the Philippines were points of contention between many Filipinos and Americans. Since the closing of the bases in 1991, relations between the United States and the Philippines have improved. Very large numbers of Filipinos have visited the U.S., and it is not uncommon to meet Filipinos who have close relatives who are U.S. citizens.

In general, there is a large amount of interest, goodwill, and understanding concerning Americans and American culture. There is also extensive understanding for volunteerism and community development that exists in Philippine national life. Many Filipinos do volunteer work in their own communities, and a large number of Filipinos have had some connection with development projects. These are great assets for Volunteers who wish to establish friendly and cooperative relationships with Filipinos. By nature, Filipinos are warm, friendly, welcoming, and are deeply concerned about the well-being of their community. The rewards of serving as a Peace Corps Volunteer in the Philippines are unlimited.

PEACE CORPS TRAINING

Overview of Pre-Service Training

The Peace Corps uses a competency-based training approach throughout the continuum of learning, supporting you from arrival in the Philippines to your departure. Pre-service training (PST) is the first event within this continuum of learning and ensures that you are equipped with the knowledge, skills, and attitudes to effectively perform your job. Pre-service training is conducted in the Philippines by Peace Corps staff, most of whom are locally hired trainers. Peace Corps staff measure achievement of learning and determine if you have successfully achieved competencies, including language standards, for swearing-in as a Peace Corps Volunteer.

Peace Corps training incorporates widely accepted principles of adult learning and is structured around the experiential learning cycle. Successful training results in competence in various technical, linguistic, cross-cultural, health, and safety and security areas.

Integrating into the community is one of the core competencies you will strive to achieve both in PST and during the first several months of service. Successful sustainable development work is based on the relationships you build by respectfully integrating into the host country community and culture.

You will be prepared for this through a homestay experience, which requires trainees to live with host families during PST. Integration into the community fosters language and cross-cultural learning and ensures your health, safety, and security.

Pre-service training is conducted during new Volunteers' first 11 weeks in the Philippines. The goal of pre-service training is to provide all Volunteers with technical, language, intercultural, safety and security, and personal and health management skills that are needed to work effectively and live successfully in Philippine sites.

Pre-service training is a combination of community- and center-based training. The first two weeks will take place at a centrally located training facility while the remainder will be conducted at cluster sites in Philippine communities. At each cluster site, which is based on project sector, the new Volunteers live with host families and train every day with four or five other trainees. The training is delivered by Philippine language, culture, and technical facilitators who live at the cluster locations in close proximity to new Volunteers.

Technical Training

Technical training will prepare you to work in the Philippines by building on the skills you already have and helping you develop new skills in a manner appropriate to the needs of the country. The Peace Corps staff, the Philippines experts, and current Volunteers will conduct the training program. Training places great emphasis on learning how to transfer the skills you have to the community in which you will serve as a Volunteer.

Technical training will include sessions on the general economic and political environment in the Philippines and strategies for working within such a framework. You will review your project's goals and objectives and will meet with the Philippines agencies and organizations that invited the Peace Corps to assist them. You will be supported and evaluated throughout training to build the confidence and skills you need to undertake your project activities, report your progress, and serve as a productive member of your community.

Technical training helps facilitate Volunteers' entry into their work assignments and their communities. Technical training sessions and activities are conducted by experienced Philippine facilitators. The purpose is to develop required technical skills and to learn about successful methods and strategies to work successfully at sites. Actual practical work in schools and community organizations is an important part of this training.

Another purpose of technical training is to help new Volunteers learn how to achieve community integration at their sites. This training includes courtesy calls to local community leaders, peer and community interviewing, community walks, field observations, community mapping, shadowing, and conducting community meetings. New Volunteers learn how to identify specific community needs and to develop strategic partnerships with community members.

Language Training

As a Peace Corps Volunteer, you will find that language skills are key to personal and professional satisfaction during your service. These skills are critical to your job performance, help you integrate into your community, and can ease your personal adaptation to the new surroundings. Therefore, language training is at the heart of the training program.

Volunteers will be trained in the national language, Filipino (Tagalog), during pre-service training. However, given that there so are many languages and dialects in the Philippines, most Volunteers learn an additional local language for two weeks in PST before moving to their permanent sites. Please note, before beginning the additional local language, Volunteers must successfully meet the minimum language requirements in Filipino (Tagalog).

Filipino language and cultural facilitators usually teach formal language classes five to six days a week in small groups. Your language training will incorporate a community-based approach. In addition to classroom time, you will be given assignments to work on outside of the classroom and with your host family. The goal is to get you to a point of basic social communication skills so you can practice and develop language skills further once you are at your site. Prior to being sworn in as a Volunteer, you will develop strategies to continue studying language during your service.

At the end of PST, all Volunteers are required to undergo an oral proficiency test called the Peace Corps Language Proficiency Interview (LPI) where every Volunteer receives a score. LPI benchmarks serve as a guide for ongoing language learning throughout service.

Volunteers are expected to commit to continued language learning. The Peace Corps supports Volunteers and offers assistance such as tutorials and language learning materials during the last few weeks of pre-service training, during the in-service training (IST) that takes place after six months, and during a weekend language intensive offered during the first year of service.

Please note, Peace Corps/Philippine Volunteers are required to take LPIs at PST, IST, mid-service training, and close of service.

Intercultural Training

Intercultural training will provide opportunities for you to reflect on your own cultural values and how they influence your behavior in the Philippines. You will also discuss the questions you have about the behaviors and practices you observe in the Philippines, exploring the underlying reasons for these behaviors and practices.

Cross-cultural and community development training will help you improve your communication skills and understand your role as a facilitator of development. Training will cover topics such as the concept of time, power and hierarchy, gender roles, communication styles, and the concept of self and relationships. Because adjusting to a new culture can be very challenging, you will participate in resiliency training which provides a framework and tools to help with adjustment issues.

The host family experience provides a unique context for intercultural learning, and is designed to ease your transition to life at your site. Families go through an orientation conducted by Peace Corps staff to explain the purpose of PST and to assist them in helping you adapt to living in the Philippines. Many Volunteers form strong and lasting friendships with their host families.

Volunteers are required to live with a host family at their site for their first three months of service and many Volunteers live with their families for the entirety of their service. A homestay debriefing is conducted during the first three months of Volunteers' service. By this time, Volunteers have been living with their host families at their permanent sites for close to two months. Some may have encountered issues or problems that should be addressed with the entire group—both for PCVs and host families. The debriefing provides the opportunity for the Volunteers and the host families to ask questions, express concerns, and discuss issues related to their host family stay with their regional manager and resource Volunteer. This debriefing session will hopefully encourage both the host families and the Volunteers to extend their homestay experience for a longer period of time. As mentioned earlier, Volunteers are strongly encouraged to continue living with host families. Usually the Volunteers who continue living with host families develop the best Philippine language fluency and the deepest understanding of Philippine culture.

Please note that independent housing can be difficult to find in some locations.

Health Training
During pre-service training, you will be trained in health prevention, basic first aid, and treatment of medical illnesses found in the Philippines. You will be expected to practice preventive health and to take responsibility for your own health by adhering to all medical policies. Trainees are required to attend all medical sessions. Health education topics will nutrition, food and water preparation, emotional health, dealing with alcohol, prevention of HIV/AIDS, sexually transmitted infections (STIs), and common illnesses in the Philippines. At the end of training, each trainee will also be asked to write a personal health plan on how they can maintain good health in country. This is a requirement prior to swearing-in.

Safety and Security Training
During the safety and security training sessions, you will learn how to adopt a lifestyle that reduces your risks at home, at work, and during your travels. You will also learn appropriate, effective strategies for coping with unwanted attention, how to identify safety risks in-country and about Peace Corps' emergency response and support systems.

Also, safety training is integrated into the language and cross-culture training activities to reflect the Volunteer reality and lifestyle. Safety training is not only for Volunteers, but is also provided for host families, Volunteers' co-workers, and supervisors.

At the end of PST, you will be tested on your knowledge, skills, and abilities on safety and security core sessions.

Additional Trainings During Volunteer Service

The Peace Corps' training system provides Volunteers with continual opportunities to examine their commitment to Peace Corps service while increasing their technical and cross-cultural skills. During service, there are usually three training events. The titles and objectives for those trainings are as follows:

- **In-service training:** Provides an opportunity for Volunteers to upgrade their technical, language, and project development skills while sharing their experiences and reaffirming their commitment after having served for three to six months.
- **Mid-service training** (done in conjunction with technical sector in-service): Assists Volunteers in reviewing their first year, reassessing their personal and project objectives, and planning for their second year of service.
- **Close-of-service conference:** Prepares Volunteers for their future after Peace Corps service and reviews their respective projects and personal experiences.

The number, length, and design of these trainings are adapted to country-specific needs and conditions. The key to the training system is that training events are integrated and interrelated, from the pre-departure orientation through the end of your service, and are planned, implemented, and evaluated cooperatively by the training staff, Peace Corps staff, and Volunteers.

Volunteers will also engage in a three-day Project Development Management training. During this training, Volunteers and their respective counterparts are taught to utilize the PDM model and have the opportunity to map out the beginning of a project they can implement in their community.

Additionally, each year Peace Corps/Philippines conducts special initiatives that include trainings and workshops. Recent trainings have included Padayon Mindanao, a cross-sectoral workshop training youth from Volunteer sites and from across the region of Mindanao in peace building and leadership. Examples of sector-specific trainings include a coral gardening workshop for Coastal Resource Management Volunteers and a maternal child health workshop for Education and CYF Volunteers.

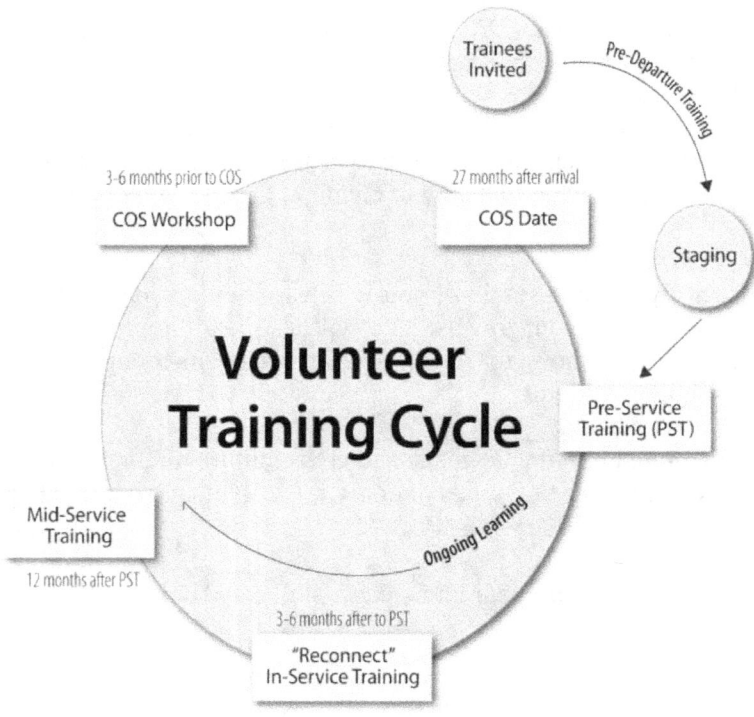

YOUR HEALTH CARE IN THE PHILIPPINES

The Peace Corps' highest priority is maintaining the good health and safety of every Volunteer. Peace Corps medical programs emphasize the preventive, rather than the curative, approach to disease. The Peace Corps in the Philippines maintains a clinic with a full-time medical officer who takes care of Volunteers' primary health-care needs, including evaluation and treatment of most medical conditions. Additional medical services are also available in the Philippines at local hospitals. If you become seriously ill and cannot receive the care you need in the Philippines, you will be transported to a Peace Corps-approved regional medical facility. If the Office of Health Services (OHS) determines that the care is not optimal for your condition at the regional facility, you will be transported to the United States.

Health Issues in the Philippines
Malaria, amebic dysentery, and other gastrointestinal illnesses, respiratory and skin infections (including fungal infections, heat rash, and heat exhaustion) are all common problems. In addition, there are occasional outbreaks of dengue fever and typhoid fever. Volunteers can decrease their risk of contracting these illnesses by practicing good health habits and following preventive measures recommended by Peace Corps/Philippines.

Note that social pressure to drink alcohol in the Philippines ranges from annoying to intolerable, and the country can be a difficult place for those who have problems controlling their use of alcohol. Peace Corps policies on conduct regarding abuse of alcohol are discussed during pre-service training.

Helping You Stay Healthy
The Peace Corps will provide you with all the necessary inoculations, medications, and information to stay healthy. Upon your arrival in the Philippines, you will receive a country-specific medical handbook. At the start of training, you will receive a medical kit with supplies to take care of mild illnesses and first aid needs. The contents of the kit are listed later in this section.

During pre-service training, you will have access to basic medical supplies through the medical officer. However, during this time, you will be responsible for your own supply of prescription drugs and any other specific medical supplies you require, as the Peace Corps will not order these items during training. Please bring a three-month supply of any prescription drugs you use, since they may not be available here and it may take several months for shipments to arrive.

You will have physicals at mid-service and at the end of your service. If you develop a serious medical problem during your service, the medical officer in the Philippines will consult with the Office of Health Services in Washington, D.C., or a regional medical officer. If it is determined that your condition cannot be treated in the Philippines, you may be sent out of the country for further evaluation and care.

Maintaining Your Health
As a Volunteer, you must accept considerable responsibility for your own health. Proper precautions will significantly reduce your risk of serious illness or injury. The adage "An ounce of prevention is worth a pound of cure" becomes extremely important in areas where diagnostic and treatment facilities are not up to the standards of the United States. The most important of your responsibilities in the Philippines is to take the following preventive measures:

Because malaria exists in the Philippines, Volunteers are required to take prophylactic medicine against the disease. Volunteers should not stop any Chemoprophylactic regimen without consulting the medical officer. Improper self-discontinuation of prophylaxis places Volunteers at risk for malaria. Volunteers who are unable to comply with malaria prevention strategies due to willful misconduct or disregard for the Peace Corps Volunteer Health Program, will be referred to the Country Director for administrative action. Those who live in areas where there is high incidence of malaria and with chloroquine resistance must take one 250 mg tablet of Mefloquine once a week or one 100 mg Doxycycline tablet daily. Those in areas with low incidence or that are malaria-free must take one 500 mg tablet of chloroquine phosphate once a week. Volunteers who cannot take any of these drugs must notify the medical officer right away for possible alternative drugs.

Many illnesses that afflict Volunteers worldwide are preventable if proper food and water precautions are taken. These illnesses include food poisoning, parasitic infections, hepatitis A, dysentery, tapeworms, and typhoid fever. Your medical officer will discuss specific standards for water and food preparation in the Philippines during pre-service training.

Abstinence is the most effective way to prevent infection with HIV and other STIs. You are taking risks if you choose to be sexually active. To lessen risk, use a condom every time you have sex. Whether your partner is a host country citizen, a fellow Volunteer, or anyone else, do not assume this person is free of HIV/AIDS or other STIs. You will receive more information from the medical officer about this important issue.

Volunteers are expected to adhere to an effective means of birth control to prevent an unplanned pregnancy. Your medical officer can help you decide on the most appropriate method to suit your individual needs. Contraceptive methods are available without charge from the medical officer.

It is critical to your health that you promptly report to the medical office or other designated facility for scheduled immunizations, and that you let the medical officer know immediately of significant illnesses and injuries.

Women's Health Information
If you require a specific product, please bring the sufficient supplies with you. Many female Volunteers take menstrual cups (The Diva Cup, The Keeper, The Moon Cup, etc.) to avoid potential problems with availability or disposal of feminine hygiene products. Feminine hygiene products such as sanitary pads and panty liners are widely available in shops and supermarkets. Tampons, however, are found mostly in big cities, but even then, may not be available in all urban supermarkets.

Pregnancy is treated in the same manner as other Volunteer health conditions that require medical attention. The Peace Corps is responsible for determining the medical risk and the availability of appropriate medical care if the Volunteer chooses to remain in-country. Given the circumstances under which Volunteers live and work in Peace Corps countries, it is rare that the Peace Corps' medical standards for continued service during pregnancy can be met.

The Peace Corps follows the 2012 U.S. Preventive Services Task Force guidelines for screening PAP smears, which recommend women aged 21–29 receive screening PAPs every three years and women aged 30–65 receive screening PAPs every five years. As such, most Volunteers will not receive a PAP during their service, but can use Peace Corps supplied health insurance after service to have an exam.

Your Peace Corps Medical Kit
The Peace Corps medical officer will provide you with a kit containing basic items to prevent and treat illnesses that may occur during service. Kit items can be periodically restocked at the medical office.

Medical Kit Contents

First Aid Handbook
Ace bandages
Acetaminophen (Tylenol)
Adhesive tape
Antacid tablets
Anti-diarrheal (Imodium)
Antibiotic ointment
Antifungal cream
Antihistamine
Antiseptic antimicrobial skin cleaner
Band-Aids
Bismuth Subsalicylate (Pepto-Bismol)
Butterfly closures
Calagel anti-itch gel
Condoms
Cough lozenges

Decongestant
Dental floss
Gloves
Hydrocortisone cream
Ibuprofen
Insect repellent
Iodine tablets (for water purification)
Lip balm
Oral rehydration salts
Scissors
Sore throat lozenges
Sterile eye drops
Sterile gauze pads
Sunscreen
Thermometer (Temp-a-dots)
Tweezers

Before You Leave: A Medical Checklist

If there has been any change in your health—physical, mental, or dental—since you submitted your examination reports to the Peace Corps, you must immediately notify the Office of Health Services (OHS). Failure to disclose new illnesses, injuries, allergies, or pregnancy can endanger your health and may jeopardize your eligibility to serve.

If your dental exam was done more than a year ago, or if your physical exam is more than two years old, contact OHS to find out whether you need to update your records. If your dentist or Peace Corps dental consultant has recommended that you undergo dental treatment or repair, you must complete that work and make sure your dentist sends requested confirmation reports or X-rays to the Office of Health Services. Dental cleaning is provided twice only during service—at mid-service and at close of service.

If you wish to avoid having duplicate vaccinations, contact your physician's office to obtain a copy of your immunization record and bring it to your pre-departure orientation. If you have any immunizations (other than yellow fever vaccination as directed by OHS) prior to Peace Corps service, the Peace Corps cannot reimburse you for the cost. The Peace Corps will provide all the immunizations necessary for your overseas assignment, either at your pre-departure orientation or during your first six months in the Philippines. Volunteers must be willing to get all required vaccinations unless there is a documented medical contraindication. Failure to accept required vaccination is grounds for administrative separation from the Peace Corps. You do not need to begin taking malaria medication prior to departure.

Bring a three-month supply of any prescription or over-the-counter medication you use on a regular basis, including birth control pills. Although the Peace Corps cannot reimburse you for this three-month supply, it will order refills during your service. While awaiting shipment—which can take several months—you will be dependent on your own medication supply. The Peace Corps will not pay for herbal or non-prescribed medications, such as St. John's wart, glucosamine, selenium, or antioxidant supplements. Medications supplied may be generic or equivalent to your current medications (including birth control pills).

You are encouraged to bring copies of medical prescriptions signed by your physician. This is not a requirement, but they might come in handy if you are questioned in transit about carrying a three-month supply of prescription drugs.

If you wear eyeglasses, bring two pairs (of the current prescription) with you. If a pair breaks, the Peace Corps will replace them, using the information your doctor in the United States provided on the eyeglasses form during your examination. The Peace Corps Office of Health Services strongly discourages Volunteers from wearing contact lenses while overseas unless there is a true medical indication documented by your ophthalmologist. Contact lenses, particularly extended use soft contacts, are associated with a variety of eye infections and other inflammatory problems. One of the most serious of these problems is infectious keratitis which can lead to severe cornea damage which could result in permanent blindness requiring corneal transplantation. These risks of permanent eye damage are exacerbated in the Peace Corps environment where the Volunteer's ability to properly clean the lenses is compromised due to limited access to sterile water as well as decreased effectiveness of cleaning solutions due to prolonged storage in unsatisfactory conditions. In addition, when bacterial eye infections occur, assessment and treatment within hours by a competent ophthalmologist is indicated. This is virtually impossible in the Peace Corps setting. If you feel that you simply must be able to use your contacts occasionally, please consider using single use, daily disposable lenses which do not require cleaning.

If you are eligible for Medicare, are over 50 years of age, or have a health condition that may restrict your future participation in health-care plans, you may wish to consult an insurance specialist about unique coverage needs before your departure. The Peace Corps will provide all necessary health care from the time you leave for your pre-departure orientation until you complete your service. When you finish, you will be entitled to the post-service health-care benefits described in the Peace Corps Volunteer Handbook. You may wish to consider keeping an existing health plan in effect during your service if you think age or pre-existing conditions might prevent you from re-enrolling in your current plan when you return home.

SAFETY AND SECURITY IN DEPTH

Ensuring the safety and security of Volunteers is Peace Corps' highest priority. Serving as a Volunteer overseas entails certain safety and security risks. Living and traveling in an unfamiliar environment, a limited understanding of the local language and culture, and the perception of being a wealthy American are some of the factors that can put a Volunteer at risk. Property theft and burglaries are not uncommon. Incidents of physical and sexual assault do occur, although most Volunteers complete their two years of service without a serious safety and security incident. Together, the Peace Corps and Volunteers can reduce risk, but cannot truly eliminate all risk.

Beyond knowing that the Peace Corps approaches safety and security as a partnership with you, it might be helpful to see how this partnership works. The Peace Corps has policies, procedures, and training in place to promote your safety. The Peace Corps depends on you to follow those policies and to put into practice what you have learned. An example of how this works in practice—in this case to help manage the risk and impact of burglary—follows:

- The Peace Corps assesses the security environment where you will live and work.
- The Peace Corps inspects the house where you will live according to established security criteria.
- The Peace Corps ensures you are welcomed by host country counterparts or other community leaders in your new community.
- The Peace Corps responds to security concerns that you raise.
- You lock your doors and windows.
- You adopt a lifestyle appropriate to the community where you live.
- You alternate your schedule or route through the neighborhood
- You avoid showing off any valuable items to community members, like tablets or computers
- You get to know your neighbors.
- You decide if purchasing personal articles insurance is appropriate for you.
- You don't change residences before being authorized by the Peace Corps.
- You communicate your concerns to Peace Corps staff.

This welcome book contains sections on Living Conditions and Volunteer Lifestyle, Peace Corps Training, Your Health Care, and Safety and Security, all of which include important safety and security information to help you understand this partnership. The Peace Corps makes every effort to give Volunteers the training and tools they need to function in the safest way possible and prepare for the unexpected, teaching you to identify, reduce, and manage the risks you may encounter.

Factors that Contribute to Volunteer Risk

There are several factors that can heighten a Volunteer's risk, many of which are within the Volunteer's control. By far the most common crime that Volunteers experience is theft. Thefts often occur when Volunteers are away from their sites, in crowded locations (such as markets or on public transportation), and when leaving items unattended.

Before you depart for the Philippines there are several measures you can take to reduce your risk:
- Leave valuable objects in the United States, particularly those that are irreplaceable or have sentimental value
- Leave copies of important documents and account numbers with someone you trust in the States
- Purchase a hidden money pouch or "dummy" wallet as a decoy
- Purchase personal articles insurance

After you arrive in the Philippines, you will receive more detailed information about common crimes, factors that contribute to Volunteer risk, and local strategies to reduce that risk. For example, Volunteers in the Philippines learn to do the following:

- Choose safe routes and times for travel, and travel with someone trusted by the community whenever possible
- Make sure one's personal appearance is respectful of local customs
- Avoid high-crime areas
- Know the local language to get help in an emergency
- Make friends with local people who are respected in the community
- Be careful and conscientious about using electronics (phones, cameras, laptops, iPods, etc.) in public or leaving them unattended
- Limit alcohol consumption

As you can see from this list, you must be willing to work hard and adapt your lifestyle to minimize the potential for being a target for crime. As with anywhere in the world, crime occurs in the Philippines. You can reduce the risks by avoiding situations that place you at risk and by taking precautions. Crime at the village or town level is less frequent than in the large cities; people know each other and generally are less likely to steal from their neighbors. Tourist attractions in large towns are favorite worksites for pickpockets.

The following are other security concerns in the Philippines of which you should be aware:

- Theft, robbery, and mugging
- Crimes related to illegal drugs
- Natural disasters such as volcanic eruptions, typhoons, and earthquakes
- Transportation-related accidents such as capsized boats and vehicle and bicycle accidents

Staying Safe: Don't Be a Target for Crime

Because many Volunteer sites are in rural, isolated settings, you must be prepared to take on a large degree of responsibility for your own safety. To reduce the likelihood that you will become a victim of crime, you can take steps to make yourself less of a target such as ensuring your home is secure and developing relationships in your community. While the factors that contribute to your risk in the Philippines may be different, in many ways you can do what you would do if you moved to a new city anywhere: Be cautious, check things out, ask questions, learn about your neighborhood, know where the more risky locations are, use common sense, and be aware. You can reduce your vulnerability to crime by integrating into your community, learning the local language, acting responsibly, and abiding by Peace Corps policies and procedures. Serving safely and effectively in the Philippines will require that you accept some restrictions on your current lifestyle.

Volunteers tend to attract a lot of attention both in large cities and at their sites, but they are more likely to receive negative attention in highly populated centers, and away from their support network ("family," friends, and colleagues) who look out for them. While whistles and exclamations may be fairly common on the street, this behavior can be reduced if you dress conservatively, abide by local cultural norms, and do not respond to unwanted attention. In addition, keep your money out of sight by using an undergarment money pouch, the kind that hangs around your neck and stays hidden under your shirt or inside your coat. Do not keep your money in outside pockets of backpacks, in coat pockets, or in fanny packs. And always walk with a companion at night.

Support from Staff

If a trainee or Volunteer is the victim of a safety and security incident, Peace Corps staff is prepared to provide support. All Peace Corps posts have procedures in place to respond to incidents of crime committed against Volunteers. The first priority for all posts in the aftermath of an incident is to ensure the Volunteer is safe and receiving medical treatment as needed. After assuring the safety of the Volunteer, Peace Corps staff response may include reassessing the Volunteer's worksite and housing arrangements and making any adjustments, as needed. In some cases, the nature of the incident may necessitate a site or housing transfer. Peace Corps staff will also support and assist Volunteers who choose to make a formal complaint with local law enforcement. It is very important that a Volunteer reports an incident when it occurs. The reasons for this include obtaining medical care and emotional support, enabling Peace Corps staff to assess the situation to determine if there is an ongoing safety and security concern, protecting peer Volunteers and preserving the right to file a complaint. Should a Volunteer decide later in the process to file a complaint with law enforcement, this option may be compromised if evidence was not preserved at the time of the incident.

Office of Victim Advocacy

The Office of Victim Advocacy (OVA) is a resource to Volunteers who are victims of crime, including sexual assault and stalking. Victim advocates are available 24 hours a day, seven days a week to help Volunteers understand their emotional, medical, and legal options so they may make informed decisions to meet their specific needs. The OVA provides a compassionate, coordinated, and supportive response to Volunteers who wish to access Peace Corps support services.

Contact information for the Office of Victim Advocacy
Direct phone number: 202.692.1753
Toll-free: 855.855.1961 ext. 1753
Duty phone: 202.409.2704 (available 24/7, call or text)
Email: victimadvocate@peacecorps.gov

Crime Data for the Philippines

Crime data and statistics for the Philippines, which are updated yearly, are available at the following link: http://files.peacecorps.gov/manuals/countrydata/philippines.pdf. Please take the time to review this important information.

Few Peace Corps Volunteers are victims of serious crimes. Crimes that do occur abroad are investigated and prosecuted by local jurisdictional authorities. If you are the victim of a crime, you will decide if you wish to file a complaint with law enforcement, who will then determine whether to prosecute. If you decide to file a complaint, the Peace Corps will help through the process. The Peace Corps staff will ensure you are fully informed of your options and understand how the local legal process works. Further, the Peace Corps will help you exercise your rights to the fullest extent possible under the laws of your host country.

The Peace Corps will train you on how to respond if you are the victim of a serious crime, including how to get to a safe location quickly and contact your Peace Corps office. It's important that you notify the Peace Corps as soon as you can so Peace Corps staff can provide assistance.

Volunteer Safety Support in the Philippines

The Peace Corps' approach to safety is a five-pronged plan to help you stay safe during your service. The plan includes information sharing, Volunteer training, site selection criteria, a detailed emergency action plan, and protocols for addressing safety and security incidents. Philippines' in-country safety program is outlined below.

The Peace Corps/Philippines office will keep you informed of any issues that may impact Volunteer safety through **information sharing**. Regular updates will be provided in Volunteer newsletters and in memorandums from the country director. In the event of a critical situation or emergency, you will be contacted through the emergency communication network. An important component of the capacity of Peace Corps to keep you informed is your buy-in to the partnership concept with the Peace Corps staff. It is expected that you will do your part to ensure that Peace Corps staff members are kept apprised of your movements in-country so they are able to inform you.

Volunteer training will include sessions on specific safety and security issues in the Philippines. This training will prepare you to adopt a culturally appropriate lifestyle and exercise judgment that promotes safety and reduces risk in your home, at work, and while traveling. Safety training is offered throughout service and is integrated into the language, cross-cultural aspects, health, and other components of training. You will be expected to successfully complete all training competencies in a variety of areas, including safety and security, as a condition of service.

Certain **site selection criteria** are used to determine safe housing for Volunteers before their arrival. The Peace Corps staff works closely with host communities and counterpart agencies to help prepare them for a Volunteer's arrival and to establish expectations of their respective roles in supporting the Volunteer. Each site is inspected before the Volunteer's arrival to ensure placement in appropriate, safe, and secure housing and worksites. Site selection is based, in part, on any relevant site history; access to medical, banking, postal, and other essential services; availability of communications, transportation, and markets; different housing options and living arrangements; and other Volunteer support needs.

You will also learn about Peace Corps/Philippines's **detailed emergency action plan,** which is implemented in the event of civil or political unrest or a natural disaster. When you arrive at your site, you will complete and submit a site locator form with your address, contact information, and a map to your house. If there is a security threat, you will gather with other Volunteers in the Philippines at predetermined locations until the situation is resolved or the Peace Corps decides to evacuate.

Finally, in order for the Peace Corps to be fully responsive to the needs of Volunteers, it is imperative that Volunteers immediately report any safety and security incidents to the Peace Corps office. The Peace Corps has established **protocols for addressing safety and security incidents** in a timely and appropriate manner, and it collects and evaluates safety and security data to track trends and develop strategies to minimize risks to current and future Volunteers.

DIVERSITY AND INCLUSION OVERVIEW

The Peace Corps mission is to promote world peace and friendship and to improve people's lives in the communities where Volunteers serve. Instituting policies and practices to support a diverse and inclusive work and Volunteer environment is essential to achieving this mission.

Through inclusive recruitment and retention of staff and Volunteers, the Peace Corps seeks to reflect the rich diversity of the United States and bring diverse perspectives and solutions to development issues. Additionally, ensuring diversity among staff and Volunteers enriches interpersonal relations and communications for the staff work environment, the Volunteer experience, and the communities in which Volunteers serve.

The Peace Corps defines diversity as a "collection of individual attributes that together help agencies pursue organizational objectives efficiently and effectively. These include, but are not limited to, characteristics such as national origin, language, race, color, disability, ethnicity, gender, age, religion, sexual orientation, gender identity, socioeconomic status, veteran status, and family structures. Diversity also encompasses differences among people concerning where they are from and where they have lived and their differences of thought and life experiences."

We define inclusion as a "culture that connects each [staff member and Volunteer] to the organization; encourages collaboration, flexibility, and fairness; and leverages diversity throughout the organization so that all individuals are able to participate and contribute to their full potential." The Peace Corps promotes inclusion throughout the lifecycle of Volunteers and staff. When staff and Volunteers are able to share their rich diversity in an inclusive work environment, the Peace Corps mission is better fulfilled. More information about diversity and inclusion can be found in the Volunteer Handbook.

An inclusive agency is one that seeks input from everyone in an effort to find the best ideas and strategies possible to execute its objectives. When input is solicited, heard, and considered from a rich multitude of individuals the best course of action usually emerges. The Peace Corps seeks to improve its operations and effectiveness by ensuring that all voices and ideas are heard and that all Volunteers and staff feel welcome and appreciated. When each person's voice is heard, the agency is stronger and the impact of Volunteers is strengthened.

Diversity and Inclusion at Your Site

Once Volunteers arrive at their sites, diversity and inclusion principles remain the same but take on a different shape, in which your host community may share a common culture and you—the Volunteer—are the outsider. You may be in the minority, if not the sole American like you, at your site. You will begin to notice diversity in perspectives, ethnicity, age, depth of conversation, and degree of support you may receive. For example, elders, youth, and middle-aged individuals all have unique points of views on topics you may discuss, from perspectives on work, new projects, and social engagements to the way community issues are addressed.

Peace Corps staff in your host country, recognize the additional adjustment issues that come with living and working in new environments and will provide support and guidance to Volunteers. During pre-service training, a session will be held to discuss diversity and inclusion and how you can serve as an ally for your peers, honoring diversity, seeking inclusion, challenging prejudice and exclusion, exploring your own biases, and learning mechanisms to cope with these adjustment issues. The Peace Corps looks forward to having Volunteers from varied backgrounds that include a variety of races, ethnic groups, ages, religions, sexual orientations and gender identities. The agency expects you to work collaboratively to create an inclusive environment that transcends differences and finds common ground.

Peace Corps Philippines Diversity Committee

Peace Corps staff leads a Diversity Committee made up of Volunteers who work together to promote an understanding of diversity issues within Volunteers, trainees, Peace Corps staff, and the communities where Volunteers serve. The committee endeavors to provide emotional and social support for trainees and Volunteers on diversity issues. The diversity committee also helps Volunteers teach diversity issues to their communities through interaction and education. Confidential, informal peer support is available to all trainees and Volunteers. The committee also develops projects that will educate Filipinos about the different issues of diversity, promoting interaction and understanding.

Cross-Cultural Considerations

Outside of Philippines' capital, residents of rural communities might have had little direct exposure to other cultures, races, religions, and lifestyles. What people view as typical U.S. behavior or norms may be a misconception, such as the belief that all Americans are rich and have blond hair and blue eyes. The people of the Philippines are known for their generous hospitality to foreigners; however, members of the community where you will live may display a range of reactions to cultural differences that you present.

As a Volunteer and representative of the United States, you are responsible not only for sharing the diversity of U.S. culture (to include your individual culture and the culture of other Americans) with your host country national counterparts, but also for learning from the diversity of your host country. An important aspect of this cultural exchange will be to demonstrate inclusiveness within your community in a sensitive manner. Additionally, you will share the responsibility of learning about the diversity of your fellow Peace Corps Volunteers and exploring how best to respect differences while serving as supportive allies as you go through this challenging new experience.

To ease the transition and adapt to life in your host country, you may need to make some temporary, yet fundamental, compromises in how you present yourself as an American and as an individual. For example, female trainees and Volunteers may not be able to exercise the independence they have in the United States; male Volunteers may be expected to not perform chores or other tasks ascribed to women; political discussions need to be handled with great care; and some of your personal beliefs may best remain undisclosed. You will need to develop techniques and personal strategies for coping with these and other limitations. The Peace Corps staff will lead a diversity, inclusion, and sensitivity discussion during pre-service training and will be on call to provide support. This training covers how to adapt personal choices and behavior to be respectful of the host country culture, which can have a direct impact on how Volunteers are viewed and treated by their new communities. The Peace Corps emphasizes professional behavior and cross-cultural sensitivity among volunteers and within their communities to help integrate and be successful during service.

An ideal way to view the pursuit of cross-cultural adaptation and/or cultural integration is to recognize that everything done in your host country has both a specific reason for why it is done and an expected outcome. Trust that your host country counterparts are acting with positive intentions and work to mutually seek understanding and commonality. Language differences may add a communication barrier and lead to misunderstandings. Listen more than you speak and seek clarity. Remember that having the ability to laugh at yourself and at life's little surprises goes a long way—laughter is universal.

Volunteer Comment
"One of the core expectations of being a Peace Corps Volunteer is being able to share parts of your culture from the United States within the community where you serve. When it comes to issues of diversity or a reality that is not in line with what a lot of people here in the Philippines think of as a 'typical American,' sometimes this sharing can be a very difficult experience. However, it has almost always been worthwhile.

"Sharing pictures of my family back in the United States with my host family and work community here has helped initiate really great conversations, mainly with kids and youth about beauty standards. It allows them to question and think about both what they have been told about people from the United States, as well as what they have been told about the beauty image they themselves are expected to uphold. Not every day and not every conversation is easy, or makes the kind of impact I would like. Some days being of a diverse family, religion, and gender standard makes the day so much more challenging and I don't leave every interaction or conversation happy with the way it went or ended. However, at the end of the day, the important thing is that I keep trying and I keep having those conversations.

"Along the way, I learn about the people I am talking to and the cultural lens they are experiencing our conversation through and I learn better ways to communicate and better ways to build important and lasting relationships, despite the differences between ourselves. This is what makes the hard days worthwhile and motivates me to continue talking, sharing, listening, and learning."

What Might a Volunteer Face?

Possible Gender Role Issues
Gender is a set of socially constructed roles, responsibilities, behaviors, and opportunities. Gender differs from sex, which refers specifically to biological and physiological characteristics of males and females. Gender roles and expectations are learned, change over time, and vary within and among cultures. Volunteers are trained in gender awareness as they approach their work in the host country. Gender roles in the United States may differ greatly from those in your country of service. It is important to absorb and to attempt to understand the cultural nuances of gender where you are. For example, in many cultures males are held in higher regard than females and females may manage the households. In some places, females are encouraged to attend school, while in other countries females are discouraged from engaging in such activities and instead work inside or outside of the home.

During the pre-service training, trainees receive an introduction to gender awareness in their country of service, and examine their own thinking about gender roles and how this thinking has impacted them. They then learn how to analyze development projects using a gender lens to better understand gender roles in their host country and to understand how these gender roles can benefit or limit what females and males may or may not do. During their 27 months of service, Volunteers will further engage in gender trainings to understand better how their gender identity impacts who they are as females or males in the host country and how this perception influences their work and relationships.

Many American women find Philippine society chauvinistic. This includes aggressive talk and behavior by men towards women, male boasting about their conquests, female ogling unconstrained about the feelings of the girl of woman, and rude jokes with explicit sexual content and profanity.

Men are also allowed much greater freedom than women. For example, Filipinos expect female but not male Volunteers to travel with a companion. Because of depictions in the media, some Filipinos assume American women are promiscuous. Behavior by women that is considered normal in the United States— such as jogging in shorts or wearing a swimsuit to swim—may reinforce this stereotype, especially in rural areas, and may lead to sexual harassment. Female Volunteers should not wear short skirts, halter-tops, or other revealing clothing. In addition, some Filipinos may have a hard time understanding what a single woman is doing away from her family. Female Volunteers accustomed to being independent may feel overprotected and may resent encouragement from Filipinos to get married. Despite these issues, the overwhelming majority of female Volunteers feel safe and happy in the Philippines.

Volunteer Comments

"I stand out with my blond hair, blue eyes, and pale skin. The majority of the time I don't have any problems. Sure, men call out as you pass on the street, but that happens in the United States, too. I tend to dress more conservatively at work and in town than the average Volunteer, in either ankle-length skirts or pants and a short-sleeved shirt. Many female Volunteers wear knee-length skirts, shorts, and tank tops and never experience any sexual harassment. The best thing to do is gauge how your work colleagues and female members of your host family dress. When I go to a student hangout with my host sister, we have no problems when we dress in tank tops. I live in a city where there are a lot of young students—many very fashionable in tube tops and miniskirts—but in a more rural area or even in my suburban barangay that would definitely not be appropriate. By all means, bring 'going out' clothes, as there are ample opportunities to wear them at nightclubs, at Volunteer parties, and on vacation."

"You can, at times, feel very limited as a woman in the Philippines. Women here do play a very large role in society, but it seems to be an 'equal but separate' philosophy. Women rarely seem to mix casually with men, although women often bring male relatives or acquaintances for security when they go out at night. If you are out alone with a man, it is assumed that he is your boyfriend—not always a bad thing! I have been told that I am demure, which appears to be a compliment here. I have noticed that women act coy, innocent, and young for their age, but when you get to know them, they often talk about men, sex, alcohol, clothes, and gossip. So it may just be a facade. Many of the women I meet do drink or smoke, but they only do it at home or at certain establishments."

"As a female Volunteer in the Philippines, you will have issues that you may never have confronted in the United States. But here, you must be aware of them for your own safety. One issue in particular that I think people should be aware of is alcohol consumption. As a female in the Philippines, you will find out that few women drink; those who do are often viewed as 'easy.'"

"Let me share a story with you. I had been at my site for eight months, and I trusted my male supervisor—I even lived with his family. I had had drinks with him and some other friends on a few occasions at my site. I never had any problems with him, such as suggestive comments or passes, and I felt comfortable with him. Then I attended a conference with him away from my site. One evening we went out with a group of friends. But this time, he made physical advances toward me. I was scared because I thought I knew him. Fortunately, nothing serious happened, but something very easily could have. This story just goes to show you that you cannot assume that everyone always understands your actions, even after you have been at your site for many months. Don't risk being caught in a circumstance like I did. Use good judgment when you are thinking about drinking with Filipino men and ask yourself if it is really worth it."

Possible Issues for Volunteers of Color

Volunteers of color sometimes, but not always, have a different Peace Corps experience than white Volunteers. Because of limited exposure, some foreign nationals will expect to see U.S. citizens who are white. Cultures of the world do not typically envision the States as a place of rich diversity with various culturally acceptable perspectives, personalities, and characteristics. Thus, a Volunteer of color may be questioned as about their U.S. citizenship.

In places where American stereotypes and/or caste system dynamics influence perception, Volunteers of color should be mindful of the reasons for these views without creating contentious environments. All too often, host country nationals are simply unaware of the diversity of the United States and require additional information and dialogue. Direct interactions with someone new or something different can take time to get used to, but those who take the time tend to be better off. Although host country nationals may assert that the United States is made up of predominately one race, we know that is not true. If a member of your community knows of compatriots living in the United States or of notable U.S. citizens of color, you can build on this knowledge as a point of reference for discussing diversity within the States.

For Volunteers of color, the range of responses to their skin color may vary from the extremely kind to the very insensitive. In African and Latin American countries, host country nationals may say "welcome home" to African Americans or Hispanic Americans. Sometimes Volunteers expect to be "welcomed home" but are disappointed when they are not. More commonly, if a Volunteer is mistaken for a host-country national citizen, he or she is expected to behave as a male or female in that culture behaves, and to speak the local language fluently. Host country nationals are sometimes frustrated when the Volunteer does not speak the local language with ease. Conversely, some in the same country may call you a "sell out" because they feel the United States has not done enough to help with social issues. These instances can be turned into teachable moments for the Volunteer and the host country national, in which the Volunteer can ask questions surrounding perception and collaborate with respect to issues and projects at hand, while engaging in cross-cultural exchanges. All Volunteers, to include white Volunteers and those of color, should be mindful of the issues of race that are embedded in U.S. culture and within the culture in your country of service. These issues may significantly affect how Volunteers interact with fellow Volunteers and host country nationals. Being open and inclusive to everyone will improve your experience in interacting with fellow Volunteers and members of your host community.

African-American Volunteers may experience racist attitudes but are more likely to face great curiosity from Filipinos about everything from intimate habits to food preferences. All Volunteers can expect to be stared at, but African Americans may get more stares. African-American Volunteers may work or live with individuals who have no experience or understanding of black American culture. They may use offensive terms, although these are more likely to be used because of ignorance than because of malice. There are parts of the Philippines where use of the "N" word and other offensive terms is prevalent, but this is used out of ignorance or misunderstanding of such language, rather than a malicious intent.

Asian-American Volunteers may be identified more by their ethnic background than by their American citizenship. They may have to deal with Filipinos' stereotypical views about other Asian cultures (e.g., all Chinese are rich traders). Mistaken for Filipinos, on the other hand, Asian-American Volunteers may be given less assistance than other Volunteers. People may expect an Asian American to speak their language and to know local customs. By the same token, by blending in, Asian Americans may not be stared at as often as other Volunteers are.

Volunteer Comments
"Upon arrival, I was greeted with tons of questions about what I am doing here, where I am from, and where I am really from. Most of the Filipinos I encounter assume I am either Japanese or Korean; American is not usually their first guess. It takes patience to describe over and over that in America not everyone is blond and Caucasian. Sometimes a local person points out Korean tourists to me, thinking I might know them. The people of my place of assignment are savvy enough to understand that I grew up in America and that I am American regardless of what I look like. On the flip side, I do not encounter some of the things that other Volunteers experience: stares at the market, kids yelling 'Kano,' etc."

"I was a Filipino-American Volunteer in the Philippines and found that host families would have been more thrilled to host a white American. People did not believe that I was a Volunteer because, to many, Americans are either Caucasian or African. Not knowing the local dialect, I tried to communicate in English, but I was labeled as a Filipino trying to be an American. White Americans or white foreigners were afforded more respect than I was in group situations. It brought me a lot of pain to experience discrimination in my own country. Thank God I was mature enough to handle this. If given another chance to serve here, I'd do it again. The experience made me a better and stronger person, and I am more convinced than ever that I can make a difference, especially in the way some people think."

"What I find to be the biggest issue is that Filipinos associate you with your ethnicity and not your nationality—even if you explain that you were born and raised in America. It's harder for people to grasp you're American than it is for them to grasp that someone of European descent is American, for example. Just don't let it bother you; it's another cultural piece of information you can share with others. One positive thing is physically blending in more with Filipinos. Thus, you get less staring and people calling 'Hey, Joe.' However, since you are also Asian, you are expected to understand the culture—like 'blessing' an elder out of respect—more than a non-Asian."

Possible Issues for Lesbian, Gay, Bisexual, Transgender, Questioning/Queer, Ally (LGBTQA) Volunteers

For LGBTQ Volunteers: Given the Philippines traditional values, sexual orientation and non-conforming gender identities might not be discussed openly. In some cases, the LGBTQ community may be stigmatized. Mindful of the cultural norms and country-specific laws, the decision to serve openly is left to each individual Peace Corps Volunteer. Many LGBTQ Volunteers have chosen to be discreet about their sexual orientation and/or gender identity within their host communities. Some LGBTQ Volunteers have chosen to come out to community members, with a result of positive and negative reactions, while some have come out only to select Peace Corps staff and Volunteers. Dealing with questions about boyfriends, girlfriends, marriage, and children may, at times, be stressful for LGBTQ Volunteers. You may find that Philippines is a less open and inclusive environment than you have previously experienced. Please know, however, that Peace Corps is supportive of you and Peace Corps staff welcomes dialogue about how to ensure your success as an LGBTQA Volunteer. More information about serving as an LGBTQ Volunteer is available at the Lesbian, Gay, Bisexual, and Transgender Peace Corps Alumni website at lgbrpcv.org. Additionally, the Peace Corps' LGBTQ employee resource group, Spectrum, can be reached at spectrum@peacecorps.gov.

For Ally Volunteers: Peace Corps staff intends to create open, inclusive, and accepting environments. As an agency, the Peace Corps encourages Volunteers to serve as allies to their LGBTQ colleagues in order to create a safe environment.

Many LGBTQ Volunteers have served successfully in the Philippines and have very fond memories of their community and service. LGBTQA support groups may be available in your country of service, providing a network to support the needs of the Peace Corps LGBTQA community. Peace Corps staff will work with Volunteers to provide them with locally informed perspectives.

It is not uncommon to encounter obviously and openly gay men (and to a lesser extent, openly gay women) in the Philippines, but Volunteers will find that attitudes about being gay or bisexual, even among Filipino gays, are not the same as in the U.S. Denial and silence play a large role in many Filipinos' interactions with gays, lesbians, and bisexuals.

In the mindsets of conservative Filipinos who might be the parents of a Volunteer's students or the leading figures at Volunteer worksites, being openly gay or bisexual might not be compatible with the role of respected professional that Volunteers are expected to fulfill. Volunteers who are immediately open to their Philippine communities about their sexual orientation might limit their acceptability and potential for success as development workers.

Although public expressions of hatred against gays, lesbians, and bisexuals are very infrequent, gay and lesbian Volunteers must contend with a commonly held attitude among Filipinos that gays and lesbians are comic characters and fair game for teasing. The situation is so varied from place to place, that each Volunteer must decide for himself or herself the most comfortable and effective way to balance possible issues about their sexual orientation with their need to integrate successfully into a new community and gain acceptance in a new culture. Going slowly is the best approach.

Volunteer Comments
"I am a lesbian who is not out in my community. I'm not out because I will only live here for two or three years. If I were going to be here longer, I might be out, but with this short of a time commitment, it would only distract from my service. It is my choice to not be out, but at times that makes for a lonely service.

"I do feel like there are Peace Corps staff who are safe to talk to, and that's helpful. I have heard people talk about *baklas* (feminine-presenting males) in a derogatory way. I have seen kids derided and bullied about it. I know youth who are in the closet and have talked to me because they assume as an American, I will understand, and keep their secret. I wish there was more I could do for them. I encourage them and make sure they know I believe in them, but sometimes it doesn't feel like enough.

"I'm excited about the diversity committee looking to do something that will reach out to Filipinos, especially the Filipino youth. A national youth camp could address many issues about all areas of diversity within the country. And then hopefully these participants will share what they've learned and the thought of change can start happening."

Possible Issues for Volunteers with Disabilities
As part of the medical clearance process, the Peace Corps Office of Health Services determined you were physically and emotionally capable, with or without additional medical support, to perform a full tour of Volunteer service in the Philippines without a significant risk of harm to yourself or interruption of service. The Peace Corps/Philippines staff will work with disabled Volunteers to support them in training, housing, jobsites, or other areas to enable them to serve safely and effectively.

Buildings in the Philippines generally are not accessible for people with disabilities. Only a few hotels and other establishments are equipped with wheelchair ramps, although some movie houses in big cities now have toilets with big doors. These deficits are largely made up for by the sheer humanity of the people. When they see a person with a disability, Filipinos behave perfectly naturally, without ingratiating themselves in an embarrassing way. And there is always someone around with a helping hand.

Volunteer Comment
"Obviously, the experience of a Volunteer with a disability will depend on his or her disability, site, project, personality, etc. I've listed the stuff I think would be good for most people to know.
 • People in the Philippines will ask a lot of questions about your disability. They will seem very inquisitive by American standards. You might want to put together a short non-technical explanation you can give.

- While some of the larger businesses are starting to develop accessibility, it's just not available in most places, especially rural ones. You'll have to take the initiative on this. Figure out what you need, and be creative and flexible in how you arrange it. Get a carpenter to modify your living space, bring portable adaptive equipment, whatever works. Peace Corps requires imagination, adaptability and a willingness to rough it from all Volunteers, disabled or not.
- Filipinos are naturally helpful, sometimes to a rather extreme extent. This can be great, like when you're trying to figure out how to get a giant box back from the post office and the clerk grabs you a pedicab; or annoying, like when the pump-boat crew practically carries you over the gangplank without permission. If they're being overly helpful, smile and explain that it's easier for you to do it your way. If you're patient and polite, they usually will listen.
- Most Filipinos with disabilities don't travel, hold jobs, or run normal errands. They either stay home where they're looked after, or beg on the streets. As a Peace Corps Volunteer, you're probably more widely traveled, better educated, and more professionally accomplished than much of your community. Just by participating in everyday life, you're setting an example that can open minds and change attitudes. Enjoy that, it's pretty cool."

Possible Issues for Volunteer Couples

Before committing to Peace Corps service, couples should consider how different degrees of enthusiasm about Peace Corps service, adaptation to the physical and cultural environment, and homesickness will affect their lives. It can be helpful to recognize that your reactions to these issues will change throughout your service, and you may not always feel the same as your partner. You and your partner will have different jobs, different schedules, and difference societal pressures. One partner may learn the language faster than the other or have a more satisfying assignment. This can create competition and put different kinds of stress on each person. Anticipating how these pressures will affect you and your partner differently throughout your service can help you remain a source of support for each other. Making friends with other Volunteers is a critical part of fitting into the larger Volunteer culture and can also be a good way to expand your support network.

While couples will live together during their service, they will live in separate towns during their pre-service training. This is a stressful time for most Volunteers, and it can be helpful to discuss in advance how you will deal with this potential separation. Your partner can be an important source of stability but can also add stress to your training experience. You may feel torn between traveling to visit your partner and focusing on your training, your host family, and friends you have made at your training site.

Couples often face pressure from host country nationals to change their roles to conform better with traditional Philippines relationships. Filipino men and women alike will often not understand American relationship dynamics and may be outwardly critical of relationships that do not adhere to traditional gender roles. It is also helpful to think about how pressures to conform to Philippine culture can be challenging to men and women in very different ways. Considering how your partner is being affected and discussing what, if any, aspects of your relationship should be changed can help reduce stress for you both.

Possible Religious Issues for Volunteers

The Philippines is the only country in Asia with a predominantly Christian population—more than 90 percent (about 80 percent of these are Roman Catholic). Of minority religious groups, about 8 percent are Muslim and 4 percent belong to the Philippine Independent Church—a nationalist Catholic Church. The *Iglesia ni Kristo* (Church of Christ) is the largest Protestant denomination with 4 percent, while Baptists, Methodists, Mormons, Jehovah's Witnesses, and other denominations make up about 2 percent. Although Volunteers are free to exercise their personal religious beliefs, they may not engage in religious proselytizing or other activities that are against the law or would impair their effectiveness as a Volunteer.

Possible Issues for 50+ Volunteers

Older Volunteers may find their age an asset in the Philippines. They will often have access to individuals and insights that are not available to younger Volunteers. On the other hand, they will be in a distinct minority within the Volunteer population and could find themselves feeling isolated, looked up to, or ignored. Older Volunteers are often accustomed to a greater degree of independence and freedom of movement than the Peace Corps' program focus and safety and security practices allow. Pre-service training can be particularly stressful for 50+ Volunteers, whose lifelong learning styles and habits may or may not lend themselves to the techniques used. An older Volunteer may be the only older person in a group of Volunteers and initially may not feel part of the group. Younger Volunteers may look to an older Volunteer for advice and support; some find this to be an enjoyable experience, while others choose not to fill this role. Some 50+ Volunteers may find it difficult to adapt to a lack of structure and clarity in their role after having worked for many years in a very structured and demanding job.

More than younger Volunteers, older Volunteers may have challenges in maintaining lifelong friendships and dealing with financial matters from afar. They may want to consider assigning power of attorney to someone in the States.

There are also benefits to being an older Volunteer. For instance, older people are shown great respect in the Philippines. But while this will open many doors, older Volunteers may also find that they are perceived as unapproachable by younger Philippine counterparts. Service in the Philippines may also be physically harder for older Volunteers, who may, for instance, find riding in motorized, three-wheel bicycles, jeepneys, or minibuses uncomfortable or have difficulty hauling water and other supplies.

Volunteer Comments

"Of course, I can't speak for seniors in other parts of the world, but I believe the Philippines to be unique. In spite of the poverty and other problems obvious to Americans, the people here are helpful and happy. One must not take offense when asked, 'How old are you, anyway?' or when people look at you as if you came from Mars. It has been my experience that they do defer to my age when I need help of any kind. And they feel it is disrespectful to ask an older person to help with a job. It takes time and patience to convince people that you are here to initiate a project and see it through to fruition. Another aspect of being a senior Volunteer is that my peers always treated me as an equal. This was invaluable in helping me adjust and get on with my job. A few physical limitations aside, I highly recommend Peace Corps service!"

"Although I am only 61 years old, there are a few issues that need to be addressed specifically for senior citizens:
- Sleeping on the floor is OK, but it's hard to get up in the morning.
- Having to dine when called is a nuisance. I want to be accommodating, but new guys should set the rules. I finally have.
- It is important to be yourself, say why you are here, and explain what your goals are.
- Be receptive to a smile, question, whatever it is, and don't feel it's intrusive. It's only a greeting.
- You have the advantage of experience and maturity. During training, be yourself and participate in classes and after hours.

In a nutshell, be prepared for poverty, a major adjustment of lifestyle, learning to wash your own clothes, eating dried fish and rice, and becoming part of a loving, sincere, needy population that gives of themselves if you do the same."

FREQUENTLY ASKED QUESTIONS

How much luggage am I allowed to bring to the Philippines?
Most airlines have baggage size and weight limits and assess charges for transport of baggage that exceeds those limits. The Peace Corps has its own size and weight limits and will not pay the cost of transport for baggage that exceeds these limits. The Peace Corps' allowance is two checked pieces of luggage with combined dimensions of both pieces not to exceed 107 inches (length + width + height) and a carry-on bag with dimensions of no more than 45 inches. Checked baggage should not exceed 100 pounds total with a maximum weight of 50 pounds per bag.

Peace Corps Volunteers are not allowed to take pets, weapons, explosives, radio transmitters (shortwave radios are permitted), automobiles, or motorcycles to their overseas assignments. Do not pack flammable materials or liquids such as lighter fluid, cleaning solvents, hair spray, or aerosol containers. This is an important safety precaution.

What is the electric current in the Philippines?
The electric current is generally 220 volt, 60 cycles, although the voltage is often less.

How much money should I bring?
Volunteers are expected to live at the same level as the people in their community. You will be given a settling-in allowance and a monthly living allowance, which should cover your expenses. Volunteers often wish to bring additional money for vacation travel to other countries. Credit cards and traveler's checks are preferable to cash. If you choose to bring extra money, bring the amount that will suit your own travel plans and needs.

When can I take vacation and have people visit me?
Each Volunteer accrues two vacation days per month of service (excluding training). Leave may not be taken during training, the first three months of service, or the last three months of service, except in conjunction with an authorized emergency leave. Family and friends are welcome to visit you after pre-service training and the first three months of service as long as their stay does not interfere with your work. Extended stays at your site are not encouraged and may require permission from your country director. The Peace Corps is not able to provide your visitors with visa, medical, or travel assistance.

Will my belongings be covered by insurance?
The Peace Corps does not provide insurance coverage for personal effects; Volunteers are ultimately responsible for the safekeeping of their personal belongings. However, you can purchase personal property insurance before you leave. If you wish, you may contact your own insurance company; additionally, insurance application forms will be provided, and you are encouraged to consider them carefully. Volunteers should not ship or take valuable items overseas. Jewelry, watches, radios, cameras, electronics, and expensive appliances are subject to loss, theft, and breakage, and, in many places, satisfactory maintenance and repair services are not available.

Do I need an international driver's license?
Volunteers in the Philippines do not need an international driver's license because they are prohibited from operating privately owned motorized vehicles. Most urban travel is by bus or taxi. Rural travel ranges from buses and minibuses to trucks, bicycles, and lots of walking. On very rare occasions, a Volunteer may be asked to drive a sponsor's vehicle, but this can occur only with prior written permission from the country director. Should this occur, the Volunteer may obtain a local driver's license. A U.S. driver's license will facilitate the process, so bring it with you just in case.

What should I bring as gifts for Filipino friends and my host family?
This is not a requirement. A token of friendship is sufficient. Some gift suggestions include knickknacks for the house; pictures, books, or calendars of American scenes; souvenirs from your area; hard candies that will not melt or spoil; or photos to give away. As a Volunteer in the Philippines, you will come to know very quickly the word and tradition of *pasalubong*. Pasalubong can be food, toys, souvenirs, clothes, goods, etc. It's a very common practice Filipinos engage in with family members, colleagues, and friends to show appreciation and thoughtfulness when returning from a trip.

Where will my site assignment be when I finish training and how isolated will I be?
Peace Corps trainees are not assigned to individual sites until after they have completed pre-service training. This gives Peace Corps staff the opportunity to assess each trainee's technical and language skills prior to assigning sites, in addition to finalizing site selections with their ministry counterparts. If feasible, you may have the opportunity to provide input on your site preferences, including geographical location, distance from other Volunteers, and living conditions. However, keep in mind that many factors influence the site selection process and that the Peace Corps cannot guarantee placement where you would ideally like to be. Most Volunteers will live in small towns or in rural villages. Volunteers are frequently within one hour or so from another Volunteer. All Volunteers serving in the Philippines should be comfortable in/around water and comfortable with small boat travel.

How can my family contact me in an emergency?
The Peace Corps Counseling and Outreach Unit provides assistance in handling emergencies affecting trainees and Volunteers or their families. Before leaving the United States, instruct your family to notify the Counseling and Outreach Unit immediately if an emergency arises, such as a serious illness or death of a family member. The Counseling and Outreach Unit can be reached at 855.855.1961, select option 1, ext. 1470. After business hours, on weekends, and on holidays, the COU duty officer can be reached at the same number. For non-emergency questions, your family can contact your country desk staff through the main Peace Corps number: 855.855.1961.

How easy is it to call home from the Philippines?
Volunteers communicate easily with friends and family in the U.S. using a variety of social networking and other sites, including Skype and Facebook. Cellphones are also used to make and receive phone calls from the U.S. Many Volunteers utilize their Peace Corps-issued phone for texting and calling in-country while having their American phone used for data and Wi-Fi for things such as Skype or Viber.

Should I bring a cellphone with me?
It's not recommended. However, if you bring one from the United States, it should be a tri- or quad-band or 4G phone. In addition, you will have to take it to a mobile phone center to have it unlocked.

Will there be email and Internet access? Should I bring my computer?
There are Internet cafes in most capital towns and cities that charge as low as 50 cents per hour. At present, there are more than 35 Internet service providers in the Philippines. Major online providers are available and are adding lines all the time.

Most Volunteers find a laptop computer or tablet essential and it is strongly recommended that you bring one. Please be aware that having a laptop involves risks due to humidity, fluctuating current, and concern for theft. If you bring a computer or other expensive electronic equipment, you may want to have it insured before you leave the U.S.

WELCOME LETTERS FROM PHILIPPINES VOLUNTEERS

Welcome to the Philippines!

We are all so excited to you have you as a part of our Peace Corps/Philippines community and to begin this next adventure of your life. You are very lucky to have been placed in this country. It is a very diverse culture filled with people who are genuinely happy and carefree, no matter what troubles come their way. Be prepared for your soul to quickly melt as one with your host community in which you will feel the spirit of *kapwa*, or togetherness. The community problems will become your own and yours the community's. To me, this is the most beautiful aspect of the Philippines.

As you are aware, times will not always be easy or fun in the next two years (but when is that a reality anywhere you're living?). What you can expect is for your many passions to be heightened, along with constant challenges at each step forward, and a support team that will never leave you hanging. I have a few pieces of advice that have been helpful my overall service thus far:

1. Be honest from the start. It is your responsibility to see that your needs are met in order to have a productive and joyful service. This means that your fellow PCVs, Peace Corps staff, and the community members must know who you are. You'll find that Philippine people are very understanding and eager to learn about your background and beliefs. It's not fair for anyone for you to hold those back from them.
2. Don't forgo your favorite hobbies or interests. Find the time that you can fit these activities in each day or week. If it's not possible in the Philippine conditions, find something new and equally exciting to occupy your time. And your new friends will love to be included in these hobbies, if possible! Anything you can do to prevent feeling hectic and lost helps to create a successful service.
3. Once you reach site, find at least one person that you can really talk to (usually someone who is very knowledgeable of the "American Culture"). You may have a site mate, but there is no guarantee of your personal connection. You will need that one person who you can be completely open with to talk cultural matters, personal matters, and just because it's nice to have someone who will always have your back.
4. Give yourself time to adjust to the food. You may not understand it or appreciate the tastes at first, but before you know it, you will find yourself also going to the canteen daily to purchase the fresh baked lumpia, banana cubes, halo-halo, etc. and wanting rice with every meal. I promise.
5. You may get a thrill from a roller coaster type lifestyle, and you won't miss it because often your emotions will experience the quick ups and downs. But I challenge you to try to enjoy this experience more like a Ferris wheel. After all, that is how the true Pinoy experiences life, slow and easy. Before you know it, that roller coaster ride will no longer seem as appealing as it once did.

Enjoy training and get to know as many people in the Peace Corps community as possible. They will be your family for (at least) the next two years of service.

Looking forward to meeting you all,
—*Education Volunteer Batch 272*

****

Welcome!

Can you believe it? You've been invited to serve in the Philippines, a country of over 7,000 islands and many more smiling faces! From the beautiful beaches and enchanting rice terraces, it's hard to imagine a more beautiful place. The Philippines, however, is so much more than its physical beauty. The genuine kindness and generosity of Filipinos will make you feel instantly at home, despite being so far away. It is a country of seemingly endless smiles and astounding resilience in the face of many challenges. Your two years will be spent working in communities that will both challenge and amaze you. You will develop friendships with the most unlikely people, fellow PCVs included, and will be forever changed by your 27 months in the "friendliest country in the world."

I'm a Coastal Resource Management (CRM) Volunteer. I live in a rural fishing community that truly lives for, and by, the sea. I primarily work with fisherfolk organizations to improve the conditions and management of marine protected areas (MPAs), but I also lend a hand wherever I can in my wonderful community (including my role as official teacher of the electric slide). I am currently working to install coral garden nurseries and train fisherfolk on the methods of coral gardening.

My days as a CRM Volunteer are pretty fluid. One day I will be in the office writing a funding proposal or creating an educational poster and the next I could be snorkeling in an MPA looking for signs of coral bleaching. There is no typical day, or even a typical site, but with some creativity and an open mind you control the trajectory of your service. Some of my favorite memories so far have been completely unrelated to my job description. The birthday parties, fiestas, language faux pas, and, of course, Pacquiao fights are just some of the memories that have made service here so special. We can't wait to see what the Philippines has in store for you and Peace Corps/Philippines couldn't be more excited for you to join our family!

—*Coastal Resource Management Volunteer, Batch 273*

****

Mabuhay!

First off, welcome to the Peace Corps/Philippines family! I know you do not know it yet, but you have just gained about 200 new friends, and that is just in-country! Consider yourself lucky to be placed in such an incredible Peace Corps post. It's about to be a wild and crazy ride, so hang on tight. It's a journey you are never going to forget. Hold onto this energy, it's contagious.

I am pretty sure, if you are anything like I was reading these letters, I had no idea what to expect or what I was doing. I promise that all gets clearer. This journey is so hard to sum up in just a single-page letter, so I am going to start with a quote sent to me from a fellow Volunteer:

> "I know you are one of the most courageous people I have ever met. I know you have a talent for loving those around you which is something too underappreciated. You are witty, kind and made of the unbreakable stuff found in the stars and the strongest of souls."

Remember this. You are going to have days that are lower than low, and that is all a part of this. Especially in CYF. Our sector is special (I mean I do not want to brag, but it's just the truth). We see things and experience things that will bring you to the root of this culture. Many of you will be working with 4P's families, the population of this culture that is in desperate need of inspiration, hope, and a light for their future. This job is so important. This is something only you, as a Volunteer, can instill. Nobody else can do that job like you. The hard part is that this is not tangible. This is nothing you will see the results of, or even feel the results of until a while down the road.

I am a year into service, and still have days where I question my impact. But let me tell you, I promise it is there. This is what CYF is all about. We are not a sector that works individually, nor do we work for outcomes. In fact, it is not even about our success, it is about the success of each and every community member we touch. We are working together as a sector, and with the community to make a long-lasting change. We are helping people help themselves. And many times, that means that you will not be the one carrying out the project or idea: The community will. This may make you feel useless and un-needed. But take it from a Volunteer who has had this pep talk with herself on multiple bike rides back and forth to the market to find comfort foods: You are making something happen. It is your presence, your being there that is the most important thing in your service. People will laugh at your ideas and tell you no and make fun of you and your plans but that is just because they are scared. Most people have not had someone believe in them enough before to invest the time and energy you are about to invest.

Welcome to CYF! Love your community, and eats lots of lechon. Sing your heart out at videoke, and carry your umbrella every day. Embrace the lows, and cherish the heck out of the highs. Celebrate with each other, and do not be so hard on yourself. Take everything day by and drink in every crazy and ridiculous moment. Remember, all the worst things make the best stories at the end. I believe in you, and so does every staff member here.

Now, go out there and get that Philippine party started!

—*CYF Volunteer, Batch 273*

PACKING LIST

This list has been compiled by Volunteers serving in the Philippines and is based on their experience. Use it as an informal guide in making your own list, bearing in mind that each experience is individual. There is no perfect list! You obviously cannot bring everything on the list, so consider those items that make the most sense to you personally and professionally. You can always have things sent to you later. As you decide what to bring, keep in mind that you have a 100-pound weight limit on baggage. And remember, you can get almost everything you need in the Philippines.

General Clothing
- One fleece or jacket (for use on air-conditioned buses)
- Six pairs of socks
- Four or five casual cotton T-shirts (for women, nothing with a deep V)
- Four pairs of shorts that extend to mid-thigh or knee
- Two or three pairs of jeans (no rips, holes, or shredding)

Women
- Five pairs of casual pants and/or capris or skirts for work
- Six work shirts/tops (like polos)
- One nice dress or skirt and top for official, more formal occasions, such as the swearing-in ceremony and courtesy calls to government officials
- Two modest one-piece bathing suits (if one gets ruined, it is hard to find a replacement locally), board shorts, and a two-piece for vacation
- 20 pairs of underwear (anything larger than a size 8 is hard to find locally)
- Five bras (anything larger than a size 36B is hard to find locally)

Men
- Two pairs of khakis or dress pants
- Swim trunks
- Five short-sleeve button-down collared shirts and/or polos (at least one of which formal enough for dress occasions)
- 12 pairs of boxers/briefs

Shoes
- One pair of formal black shoes for important and special occasions
- One pair of comfortable dress/work shoes
- One pair of flip-flops
- Sandals with straps
- Sneakers or running shoes

Personal Hygiene and Toiletry Items
- A starter kit of travel size toiletry items that you can refill when you deem necessary.
- Tampons are not readily available and you may want to pack a large zip-top bag full
- If you have curly or kinky hair, you may want to bring a starter supply of hair products; it is difficult to find products for hair other than "Fine-straight."

Electronics
* It will be important to take good care of your electronics by keeping things dry in plastic and away from insects that could be potential hazards.

- Laptops are highly recommended
- Reader device (Kindle, Nook, or tablet)
- Earbuds or headphones
- MP3 player, iPod, music playing device (music is a big part of the culture in the Philippines)
- External hard drive for backing up files and file sharing with PCVs
- USB or flash drive
- Good quality flashlight
- Camera: Waterproof for diving, DSLR, and/or point and shoot(depending on your needs/hobbies)

Miscellaneous
- Three lightweight, super-absorbent quick-dry body towels
- Rechargeable batteries and charger (AA and AAA)
- Swiss Army knife or Leatherman tool
- Durable backpack big enough for a five-day trip
- Photos of your family, friends, and pets to show your community
- Sunglasses
- Ear plugs (useful when there's so much noise around)
- Two cotton sheets (queen-sized flat sheet only, with pillow cases)
- Small, cheap gifts for your two host families, such as Uno and other American games, U.S. maps, calendars with pictures in them (maybe of your home state), coloring books, key chains, pens and pencils, chocolate, and hard candies like Jolly Ranchers.
- Snorkel gear, especially for CRM Volunteers
- Bike helmet and removable bike light(s) (If you plan on riding a bike)

What Not To Bring
- Mosquito net (the Peace Corps issues you one upon arrival)
- Pepto, Imodium, water tablets, dental floss, bug spray, etc. The Peace Corps issues Volunteers a thorough medical kit with all this and more on the day of arrival.
- Jewelry with emotional value or anything with diamonds
- Spices for cooking. Spices could be construed as an agricultural product and importation restrictions may apply.
- Short-wave radio. There are legal restrictions related to the use of short wave radios in the Philippines.

PRE-DEPARTURE CHECKLIST

The following list consists of suggestions for you to consider as you prepare to live outside the United States for two years. Not all items are relevant to everyone, and the list is not comprehensive.

Family
- Notify family that they can call the Counseling and Outreach Unit at any time if there is a critical illness or death of a family member (24-hour phone number: 855.855.1961 ext. 1470).
- Give family and friends the Peace Corps On the Home Front handbook.

Passport/Travel
- Forward to the Peace Corps travel office all paperwork for the Peace Corps passport and visas.
- Verify that your luggage meets the size and weight limits for international travel.
- Obtain a personal passport if you plan to travel after your service ends. (Your Peace Corps passport will expire three months after you finish service; if you plan to travel longer, you will need a regular passport.)

Medical/Health
- Complete any needed dental and medical work.
- If you wear glasses, bring two pairs.
- Arrange to bring a three-month supply of all medications (including birth control pills) you are currently taking.

Insurance
- Make arrangements to maintain life insurance coverage.
- Arrange to maintain supplemental health coverage while you are away. (Even though the Peace Corps is responsible for your health care during Peace Corps service abroad, it is advisable for people who have pre-existing conditions to arrange for the continuation of their supplemental health coverage. If there is a lapse in coverage, it is often difficult and expensive to be reinstated.)
- Arrange to continue Medicare coverage if applicable.

Personal Papers
- Bring a copy of your certificate of marriage or divorce.

Voting
- Register to vote in the state of your home of record. (Many state universities consider voting and payment of state taxes as evidence of residence in that state.)
- Obtain a voter registration card and take it with you overseas.
- Arrange to have an absentee ballot forwarded to you overseas.

Personal Effects
- Purchase personal property insurance to extend from the time you leave your home for service overseas until the time you complete your service and return to the United States.

Financial Management
- Keep a bank account in your name in the United States.
- Obtain student loan deferment forms from the lender or loan service. Information about loan deferment is online at peacecorps.gov/loans/.
- Execute a power of attorney for the management of your property and business.

- Arrange for deductions from your readjustment allowance to pay alimony, child support, and other debts through the Office of Volunteer Financial Operations at 855.855.1961 ext. 1770.
- Place all important papers—mortgages, deeds, stocks, and bonds—in a safe deposit box or with an attorney or other caretaker.

CONTACTING PEACE CORPS HEADQUARTERS

This list of numbers will help connect you with the appropriate office at Peace Corps headquarters to answer various questions. You can use the toll-free number and extension or dial directly using the local numbers provided. Be sure to leave the toll-free number and extensions with your family so they can contact you in the event of an emergency.

Peace Corps headquarters toll-free number: 855.855.1961, press 1, then extension number (see below)

Peace Corps mailing address:

Peace Corps
Paul D. Coverdell Peace Corps Headquarters
1111 20th Street NW
Washington, DC 20526

For Questions about	Staff	Toll-free extension	Direct/Local
Responding to an invitation	Office of Placement	ext. 1840	202.692.1840
Country information	Country Desk officer	ext. 2316	202.692.2316
	Desk Officer	philippines@peacecorps.gov	
Plane tickets, passports, visas, or other travel matters			
	CWT SATO Travel	ext. 1170	202.692.1170
Legal clearance:	Office of Placement	ext. 1840	202.692.1840
Medical clearance and forms processing (includes dental)			
	Screening Nurse	ext. 1500	202.692.1500
Medical Applicant Portal questions		amsadmin@peacecorps.gov	
Medical reimbursements (handled by a subcontractor)			800.544.1802
Loan deferments, taxes, financial operations		ext. 1770	202.692.1770
Readjustment allowance withdrawals, power of attorney, staging (pre-departure orientation), and reporting instructions			
	Office of Staging	ext. 1865	202.692.1865
New Volunteer Portal questions		staging@peacecorps.gov	

Note: You will receive comprehensive information (hotel and flight arrangements) three to five weeks prior to departure. This information is not available sooner.

Family emergencies (to get information to a Volunteer overseas) 24 hours			
	Counseling and Outreach Unit	ext. 1470	202.692.1470
Office of Victim Advocacy		ext. 1753	202.692.1753
		24 hours (call or text)	202.409.2704